Teaching Formation Mathematics

Teaching Foundation Mathematics

A guide for teachers of older students
with learning difficulties

Nadia Naggar-Smith

Routledge
Taylor & Francis Group

LONDON AND NEW YORK

First published 2008
by Routledge
2 Park Square, Milton Park, Abingdon, Oxon OX14 4RN

Simultaneously published in the USA and Canada
by Routledge
270 Madison Ave, New York, NY 10016

Routledge is an imprint of the Taylor & Francis Group, an informa business

© 2008 Nadia Naggar-Smith

Typeset in Helvetica by
Newgen Imaging Systems (P) Ltd, Chennai, India
Printed and bound in Great Britain by
Bell & Bain Ltd, Glasgow

British Library Cataloguing in Publication Data
A catalogue record for this book is available from the British Library

Library of Congress Cataloging in Publication Data
Naggar-Smith, Nadia.
    Teaching foundation mathematics: a guide for teachers of older students with
  learning disabilities / Nadia Naggar-Smith.
        p. cm.
      1. Mathematics – Study and teaching. 2. Learning disabled – Education. I. Title.
    QA11.2.N34 2008
    371.9′0447–dc22   2007026179

ISBN10: 0–415–45164–7 (pbk)
ISBN10: 0–203–93879–8 (ebk)

ISBN13: 978–0–415–45164–2 (pbk)
ISBN13: 978–0–203–93879–9 (ebk)

Contents

PART II
Measure   **87**

Introduction

This book has been written as a resource package for tutors of pupils or adults with moderate to severe learning difficulties. It is a progressive series of lessons, split into three main areas – Number, Measure and Shape. These are areas covered by the Adult Pre-Entry Curriculum Framework and the P Scales. It is aimed at children over twelve and adults.

Each area is divided into ten lessons and each lesson is mapped to the current criteria. Worksheets or ideas for recording progress are included for most lessons. All of the lessons have been designed so that they can be used with students in the same class who have a wide range of learning difficulties or special needs. This is also reflected in the recording of the students' progress.

The author is a tutor in adult education with several years of experience. She started her career as an accountant and contributed to courses at Liverpool University. She began to teach adults with learning difficulties on a part-time basis and gradually changed her career. She now works full time in a college in the Further Education sector. During her teaching, she has found a sparseness of readily available teaching material. The pre-GCSE resources available were often not amenable to adaptation. To help other tutors who may be experiencing similar difficulties, she has written this book. The lessons have been used many times.

The Adult Pre-entry Curriculum Framework for Literacy and Numeracy

The framework sets out the entitlement to learning numeracy for adults with learning difficulties and/or disabilities who have not yet reached Entry 1 in the Adult Numeracy core curriculum. It provides clear and detailed steps to enable learners to progress towards Entry 1 in a structured way.

(The Adult Pre-entry Curriculum Framework for
Literacy and Numeracy, DFES 2002)

The Adult Pre-entry Curriculum Framework for Numeracy has been organised as a series of eight milestones. The milestones are then broken down into broad areas of learning and teaching called elements. The elements are then broken down into sub-elements, which are smaller, 'bite-sized' areas of learning. These links between activities and Adult Pre-entry Curriculum Framework elements are represented in the publication by the abbreviation (MSS/E). The lessons and activities in this publication are mapped to the elements and sub-elements used in the Adult Pre-entry Curriculum Framework.

The P scales

The P scales are differentiated criteria. They outline attainment for pupils working below Level 1 of the mainstream national curriculum and describe some of the important skills, knowledge and understanding that pupils may gain from the programmes of study in the national curriculum.

P scales are not designed to be used to define curriculum content or as a detailed step-by-step curriculum.

(Using the P scales: Qualifications and Curriculum Authority 2005)

Each lesson in this book relates to the criteria within the P scales and the best fit level for the skills, knowledge and understanding presented is indicated in the tutor's notes.

The lessons have been designed to build a mathematics 'tool kit' for students to carry with them into the core curriculum and to use in everyday life. They can be revisited either by students working within the core curriculum who have gaps in their learning, or progressively by those who are forming a basic 'tool kit'.

The requirements of numeracy for the Adult Pre-entry Curriculum Framework may be considered to be 'elementary' in their terms of position within the hierarchy of learning mathematics; it does not follow that students will find them either simple or straightforward to learn. The mastery of each topic will depend not only on carefully constructed and well taught lessons, but also on what each student brings to the lesson in terms of ability, aptitude and previous knowledge.

The layout of the book

Within the book there are 29 complete lessons, which are progressive. Each lesson comes complete with:

* Tutor's notes and criteria specifications
* Teaching objectives
* A list of resources needed for the lessons
* A detailed lesson plan
* Photocopiable worksheets.

Included in the introduction to the book is the introduction to the topics to be taught, namely, Number (the Number Tool Kit), Measure and Shape. Handling of data is not presented as a separate element; it permeates all topics when gathering and recording information.

The lessons

The lessons have been designed to be used in two stages:

Stage 1: Introduction of topic and class discussion

Each lesson starts with a class discussion, to allow everyone to have input and allow the teacher to assess the level of prior knowledge of the topic to be covered. It helps students to focus on the learning situation and introduces the language to be used. Any apparatus to be used is also introduced at this stage.

Stage 2: The activity

During this part of the lesson students work individually, in pairs or in small groups. They are encouraged to question, answer and record. Clear instructions are given on what to do with the worksheet(s).

Length of time for lessons

The length of time taken to master a topic, or item, in mathematics is dictated by what individual students bring to the lesson in terms of learning strengths and weaknesses. In some cases one lesson is not long enough to cover the items planned; one item could even become a topic and spread over several mathematics lessons. For this reason, the length of time for each lesson has been excluded from the tutor's notes. It is unlikely that all the lessons will be covered in one academic year.

Students dictate the pace of learning; the lessons in this book have been planned to take this into consideration.

Worksheets

Worksheets enable each student, or group of students, to work at a pace best suited to their needs and can be stored in student files, as a record of individual progress.

The worksheets do not need colour, as this makes photocopying easier and less expensive. Often students like to colour things in, and although this can be time-consuming it can help them to remember. The use of fine motor skills for colouring and the introduction of colour are both multisensory activities and can help students to commit the mathematics involved to memory.

Font size and style for worksheets

Through trial and improvement the author found font size 16 the most comfortable for students to work with. This may use more paper, but students seem to be more comfortable using a larger font. Arial is a good font to use as the printed letters are more compatible with handwritten letters than those of Times New Roman, for example the letter g.

Comic Sans is also a good font style to use for variety.

The resources in this book are not definitive and may need to be supplemented with other compatible resources.

Concept development

Ideally students should move through four stages of developing abstract thinking when learning mathematics:

1   physical experience;
2   language to describe that experience;
3   representation;
4   symbolisation.

Although many adult learners will be able to combine the first and second of these stages, i.e., physical experience and language to describe it, some will not. Many students will use mathematical words without understanding, often because the pace of teaching is increased beyond the pace of learning (understanding) for them. Pace is very important in all teaching, including teaching students who have previously found learning difficult. Therefore, lessons are structured so that tutors may offer them in small steps, or in their entirety. The lessons offer opportunities for students to make links, to fill in learning gaps and to follow a structured programme, but above all they offer opportunities for students to enjoy mathematics.

Although it is important to use the correct terminology in mathematics, students should initially be allowed to use their own language, as this encourages their participation in the lesson.

Multisensory learning

We all use our five senses in different ways to help us to remember and recall facts and there are three main learning styles:

1 **Visual learners**:   who like to see things written down, look at pictures and objects and watch demonstrations. Shape and colour are also important to them.
2 **Auditory learners**: who like explanations, repeating names and words.
3 **Tactile learners**:   who like to touch things and move them around.

Students have different strengths and weaknesses in their ability to use their senses to help them to learn. It is therefore important to offer a variety of multisensory learning experiences.

Part I
Number

Introduction to Number

Numeracy

When the word 'numeracy' was first introduced in the Crowther Report in 1959, it related to a sophisticated level of mathematical understanding to be found in the sixth form curriculum and to the application of mathematics. Later, it was widely used to describe the ability to perform basic arithmetic operations. This later definition was responsible for the restricted curriculum offered to students with learning difficulties.

It was not until the publication of the Cockcroft Report, in 1982, that it was given its current meaning. This report recommended that the word 'numerate' should imply the possession of two attributes:

1   an ability to make use of mathematical skills, which enables an individual to cope with the practical mathematical demands of his or her everyday life;
2   an ability to have some appreciation and understanding of information which is presented in mathematical terms, for instance charts, tables and graphs.

In that report the basic skills for adult life are given as an ability:

- to read numbers and to count;
- to tell the time;
- to pay for purchases and to give change;
- to weigh and to measure;
- to estimate and approximate;
- to understand straightforward timetables and simple graphs and charts; and
- to carry out any necessary calculations associated with these.

Most important of all is the need to have sufficient confidence to make effective use of whatever mathematical skill and understanding is possessed, whether this be little or much.

The recommendations of the Cockcroft Report form the foundations of both the mainstream National Curriculum for Mathematics and the National Numeracy Strategy for England.

Number

The Adult Pre-entry Curriculum Framework for Numeracy aims to make students numerate to a level commensurate with their ability. The teaching and learning elements are: Number, Measure, Shape and Space, and Handling Data.

In preparation for the Adult Numeracy core curriculum, students will *work towards* mastery of the following skills:

- counting to ten;
- comparing quantities to five;
- reading, writing and ordering numerals to ten;
- counting sets of objects to ten;
- adding to ten;
- subtracting to ten;
- using ordinal numbers from first to fifth;

- understanding and applying the addition, minus and equal symbols; and
- understanding simple bar charts.

The Number lessons in this book have been carefully planned to provide students with an opportunity to build a Number Tool Kit for use in everyday life and to take with them when they progress to the core curriculum.

The Number section of this book offers suggestions for ten lessons to assist in the teaching and learning of number. Each lesson is directly linked to the Adult Pre-entry Curriculum Framework for Numeracy and the P scales.

References

Crowther Report 15 to 18 (1959): A report of the Central Advisory Council for Education England, HMSO London.

Mathematics Counts (1982): Report of the Committee of Inquiry into the Teaching of Mathematics in Schools under the Chairmanship of Dr W.H. Cockcroft, HMSO London.

Lesson N1 – Cardinal numbers

Tutor's notes

This lesson helps to develop concepts of cardinality up to five, through visualisation of quantities. Most adults, but not all, can see quantities to about six, without having to count them (subitising). Although your students should be comfortable with visual quantities up to five, you may need to adjust the number to four. Sometimes you may encounter a student with a specific learning difficulty who cannot subitise; this lesson may not be suitable for such students, but try building the activity gradually with numbers one, then two, to as far as they can go.

When preparing visual number cards, it is important not to group the spots or objects in familiar pattern forms, for example those used on dice or playing cards, as there is a possibility of students relating the quantity only to the number pattern. Patterns become important after the concept has been developed.

When using visual number cards, they remain on the overhead projector (OHP) to the silent count of three and are then withdrawn, as the presenter says, 'Say it fast'. This prompts students to visually remember what they saw.

An alternative way of using the cards is to have two students working together at the OHP. One student puts the cards down and the other takes them off. The remaining students watch the screen and say how many spots they can see, as fast as they can.

The lesson lays the foundations for mental mathematics and progresses to requiring students to hold the visual number of spots in their 'mind's eye', while adding or subtracting one. Nothing is recorded during this activity.

The worksheets encourage students to discuss, remember and record what they did during the activity. This forms a link between this visualisation and the beginning of recorded mathematics. This same systematic approach used in the mental addition activity can be used for mental subtraction. A recording sheet is included for this.

Criteria

Adult Pre-entry Curriculum Framework for Numeracy

Number

Milestone 6 – sub-element 3
Milestone 7 – sub-element 2 and sub-element 4
Milestone 8 – sub-element 3 and sub-element 6

P scales

Using and applying mathematics   P8
Number   P8

Lesson N1   Cardinal numbers

Objectives

- to recognise quantities without counting;
- to strengthen visual memory;
- to create foundations for addition and subtraction.

Resources

- A5 cards with holes punched in them:
  One set of cards comprises 5 cards with 1, 2, 3, 4 or 5 holes in them. Make a further set with the holes positioned differently.

  Alternatively, prepare squares of OHP transparencies with coloured spots on them.
- Worksheet 1 – one copy for each student;
- Worksheet 2 – one copy for each student;
- OHP and screen.

Lesson plan

Stage 1: Introduction and class discussion

1   Shuffle the spot cards.
2   Place one of the prepared spot cards on the OHP and ask students how many spots they can see.
3   Ask how they know it is two or four, or whatever number of spots is showing on the screen. Find out if they just knew, or if they counted the spots.
4   Repeat this with different cards, leaving them on the OHP while you ask how many spots they can see each time. Questions to ask are: 'Did you just know?' or 'Did you count?', 'How did you count?'.

Activity 1: Visualisation of numbers

1   Explain that you are now going to place the spot cards on the OHP, one at a time as before, but that this time they are going to have to be very fast in saying the number, because you will move the card away very quickly.
2   Place a spot card on the OHP, silently count to two and then move the card off the OHP as you ask students to, 'Say it fast'.
3   Repeat this several times and pause while you discuss how they are finding the number now – by counting or knowing.
4   Repeat until all of the cards have been used.
5   Invite students to form pairs and volunteer to be the callers. Explain that one student will place the card on the OHP and the other will call 'Say it fast' as they take the card off the OHP.

Each pair should present four or five cards.

Activity 2: Mental addition

1   Explain that you are going to do the activity again but that they will have to listen very carefully, as it is going to be a little different.
2   Repeat step 5 of Activity 1 and, after the students have given the number, ask them 'And one more?'.
3   Repeat step 2 as many times as you need to, to make the students comfortable with the pattern of the activity.
4   At this point, nothing will have been recorded and it is also not necessary to have a written record but, sometimes students like to see their activity written down. Worksheet 1 may be used to provide a written record of what students did; they may need to have the worksheets explained to them.

Extension work

The above activity for mental addition can be used for mental subtraction.

1   Follow steps 1, 3 and 4 as given for Activity 2.
2   Replace step 2 with the following:
    a   Place a spot card on the OHP and withdraw it quickly saying, 'Say it fast'.
    b   Then ask students, 'One less?'.
3   Worksheet 2 provides a means of recording what students did and should be used at this stage.

Name:_____ **Date:**_____

One More

This is what we did

Looked   **Thought**   **Answered**

and one more

and one more

and one more

and one more

Name:_____ **Date:**_____

One Less

This is what we did

Looked	**Thought**	**Answered**
	one less	
	one less	
	one less	
	one less	

Lesson N2 – Ordinal numbers

Tutor's notes

Ordinal numbers tell us the order in which items are to be counted. The suggested ordinal numbers to be taught at this stage of development are: first, second, third, fourth, fifth and last.

In Activity 1, a 'queue jumper' has been introduced to change the order of the students in the queue. You will need to make some cards for this activity. The cards should be large enough for the students to hold above their heads and should have 'First', 'Second', 'Third', 'Fourth', 'Fifth', 'Last' written on one side, and '1st', '2nd', '3rd', '4th', '5th' written on the other. Other cards with 'Last', 'Next' and 'QJ' (for queue jumper) should also be included. These could also be laminated and kept with the other resources.

A table of ordinal numbers (page 17) should be photocopied and laminated (preferably in colour). Each student should be provided with one copy of these tables. An enlarged copy should be made for tutor demonstration. Alternatively, the tutor could use an OHP or draw a table on the board.

Some students will have difficulty following a demonstration by the tutor while trying to work with the table in front of them. It is better for them if they are made familiar with the demonstration table before they are given their individual copies to work from.

Activity 2 uses TV soaps as this often promotes lively discussion about the soaps and which is everyone's favourite and why.

Criteria

Adult Pre-entry Curriculum Framework for Numeracy

Number

Milestone 7 – sub-element 7
Milestone 8 – sub-element 9

P scales

Using and applying mathematics   P8
Number   P8

Lesson N2   Ordinal numbers

Objectives

- to practice using ordinal numbers for position of people in queues and time of events;
- to read ordinal numbers;
- to write ordinal numbers.

Resources

For each pair of students:

- a copy of a page of recent television timings showing when the popular soaps are on;
- a copy of a recent football league table;
- a variety of highlighter pens;
- Worksheet 1– one copy for each student;
- Worksheet 2– one copy for each student;
- table of ordinal numbers (this could be laminated);
- cards with ordinal numbers on (see tutor's notes);
- some large Post-its (about ten).

Lesson plan

Stage 1: Introduction and class discussion

1   Write numerals 1 to 5 on the 'Post-its', and stick them at random on the board. Now ask students to read what you have written on the stickers (point to the numbers in no particular order).
2   Now explain that the numbers are all mixed up and you want to put them in order. Draw a line on the board. Ask which number should come first and invite a student to come and place the sticker on the line.
3   Now do the same with the second, third, fourth and fifth.
4   Talk about the numerals one at a time referring to the idea of their position and ordinal numbers. One student should also have a card with 'Last' on it.
5   Now introduce 'last'. Questions to ask: 'Which number is last?', 'Can this number be fifth as well as last?', 'Have you ever been last?', 'What else can be last?'. This could be related to their timetable, horse races, position in a queue, the order in which soaps are on in an evening, the position of football teams in the league and so on.

Activity 1: In the queue

For this activity you will need a set of cards with 'First', 'Second', 'Third', 'Fourth', 'Fifth', 'Last' written on one side and '1st', '2nd', '3rd', '4th', '5th' written on the other. Other cards with 'Last', 'Next' and 'QJ' should also be included (see tutor's notes).

1   Select a group of four students to form a queue.
2   Ask 'Who is first in the queue?' and give them a card with 'First/1st' on it.
3   Ask 'Who is last?' and give them a card with 'Last' on it.

4   Students should now decide which position they are in. They should then hold up the appropriate card with 2nd, 3rd and 4th, on it. One student should also have a card with 'Last' on it.
5   Discuss why the person who is fourth now has two cards.
6   Introduce Worksheet 1 and ask students 'Who is first?', 'Who is last?' and so on, and students should record the names in the boxes.
7   Select another student to be the QJ and give him or her the card with QJ on it.
8   Now QJ should join the queue in any position they choose (even if they choose to be last). This promotes interesting discussion.
9   Now ask questions such as, 'Who is first in the queue?', 'Who is third?' and so on. Students should then exchange cards if necessary. There are now five people in the queue. The card with 'Fifth/5th' on it will need to be introduced.
10   Discuss how the positions have been changed.
11   Ask students to select the appropriate cards and give them to the students whose positions have changed.
   (Steps 12 and 13 are optional)
12   With the QJ in second position, introduce Worksheet 2.
13   Ask students to fill in the blank boxes on the worksheet.
14   This activity can then be repeated with a different group of students.

Activity 2

1   Students may work individually or in pairs.
2   Give out highlighter pens and a copy of the television timings. Ask students to highlight all the soaps on that day.
3   Ask the students to write down the name of the soap that is on TV first on that day. Alternatively, there could be cards with the names of the different soaps on them.
4   Then ask them which one is second and so on.
5   Ask students to list their favourite soaps in order of preference and talk about their preferences: 'Which is the first soap on your list?' 'Which is the last soap on your list?' and so on.

Activity 3

1   Give out the football table. Ask students to highlight the first team in one colour and the third in another.
2   Using this as an oral exercise, ask students which team is second, fifth and so on.

Once you feel students are confident with ordinal numbers they should then be given Worksheet 3 to complete.

   Students should place a copy of the table of ordinal numbers on the next page in their file for future reference.

Table 1
Table of Ordinal Numbers

1	1st	FIRST
2	2nd	SECOND
3	3rd	THIRD
4	4th	FOURTH
5	5th	FIFTH

© Nadia Naggar-Smith, *Teaching Foundation Mathematics*, Routledge, 2008

Ordinal Numbers Worksheet 1

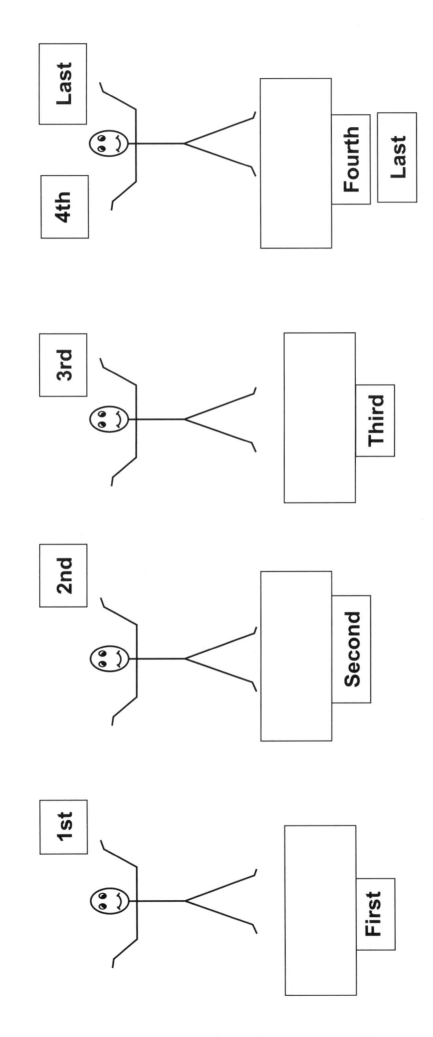

Ordinal Numbers
Worksheet 2

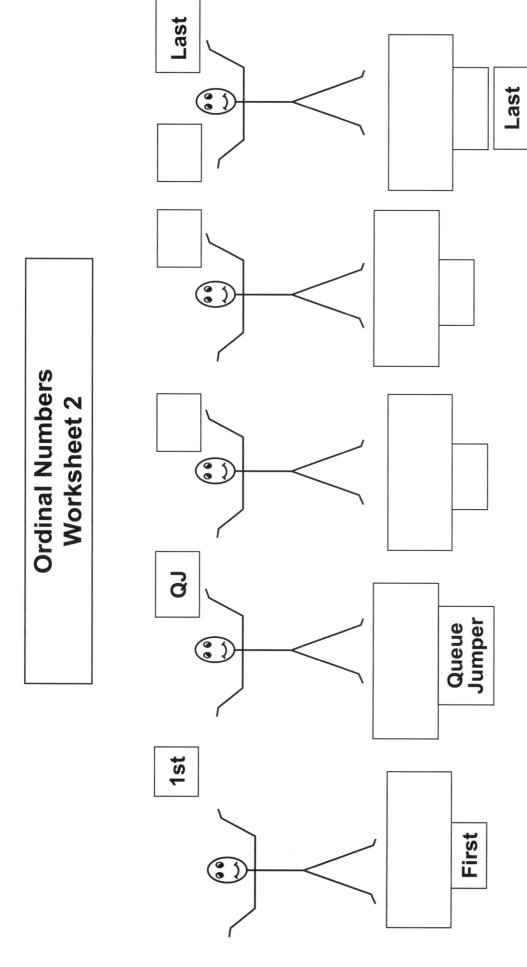

1st

QJ

Last

First

Queue Jumper

Last

Ordinal Numbers
Worksheet 3: The Sack Race

Below are the results of a local sack race for charity.

The winner was the person who completed the race in the shortest time.

Name	Time
Janet	3 minutes
Andrew	5 minutes
Michael	2 minutes
Kelly	4 minutes
Julian	10 minutes
Angus	6 minutes

Name: _____ **Date:** _____

1 Write the names in the order they finished the run, starting with the person that came first.

Name	Time

2 Who came first? _____

3 Who was fourth? _____

4 In which position did Angus finish? _____

5 Who finished in third place? _____

6 Who finished last? _____

7 Who finished in second place? _____

8 Who won the race? _____

Lesson N3 – Card bingo

Tutor's notes

This lesson has been designed to provide students with an opportunity to rehearse rapid recognition of both number symbols and quantities.

The activity is introduced as a whole class game and involves the use of ordinary playing cards Ace to 10. The use of two colours (red and black) and four different shapes (hearts, spades, clubs and diamonds) on the cards is useful in finetuning the concept that cardinality is dependant neither on colour nor shape.

Adaptations

This lesson can be adjusted to meet different learning needs, as below.

1   If your students are comfortable with the numbers 1 to 10, you will only need to remove the picture cards from the pack.
2   If your students are working with single digit numbers 1 to 9, then you will also need to remove the 10.
3   If your students are working with numbers up to 5, remove all picture cards and cards with values higher than 5.

The numeral 4 is sometimes confusing and it may be necessary to make a sticker for these cards with 4 on it. Place it so that both numerals are visible, as students will meet 4 in many other places. (The Ace may also be shown as 1, if necessary.)

If your students find it difficult to use playing cards, because they are distracted from the numbers by the patterns, you could make your own set of numbered cards with just numerals on them.

For some students, it will be useful to have a 'Bingo Board' to make it easier for them to set their cards out correctly. They could put a frame on this or colour in the boxes, to personalise it, then use the same board in future games.

The game

As with all games, it is important to familiarise students with the rules before they begin and give them the opportunity to resolve any misunderstandings. They also need to know whether they will be grouped individually or in pairs.

Students need to know:

*   how they will be grouped;
*   how to start the game;
*   how to continue the game;
*   how to finish the game.

The game can be extended by the use of rows, columns and diagonals. To demonstrate row, column and diagonal, make an OHT of Tutor Sheet 1 (p. 26).

Criteria

Adult Pre-entry Curriculum Framework for Numeracy

Number

Milestone 6 – sub-element 1, sub-element 2, sub-element 3 and sub-element 4
Milestone 7 – sub-element 1 and sub-element 3
Milestone 8 – sub-element 1 and sub-element 5

These elements progress to N1/E1.1 of the Adult Numeracy core curriculum.

P scales

Using and applying mathematics	P8
Number	P7 (numbers to 5)
	P8 (numbers to 10)

Lesson N3   Card bingo

Objectives

- to reinforce the concept of quantities;
- to aid rapid number recognition (1 to 9).

Resources

- three or four packs of playing cards, depending on the number of students taking part. (You will need nine cards per student or per group plus **your** pack containing one of each card, in red and black.);
- alternatively, number cards made for the game. (See tutor's notes, adaptation 3);
- a 'Bingo Board' (optional);
- prizes or reward scheme;
- OHT of Tutor Sheet 1.

Lesson plan

Stage 1: Introduction and class discussion

1   Sort the cards by removing all the picture cards and cards with a value above five. If your students are comfortable with numbers up to ten, you could just remove the picture cards.
2   Students may play individually or in pairs. Some students may prefer to work in pairs, to help each other with recognising numbers and colours.
3   Talk about the cards to familiarise students with them. For example, 'How many colours are there?' 'Find the card with the number 4 on it', and so on.
4   Establish the value of the ace:
     Ask students to find a card without any numbers on it. Talk about the card. Questions to ask: 'Does anyone know the name of this card?' 'What is the value of the card with the "A" on it?' 'How many shapes are there on the card?' 'What number do you think this card should be?'. Explain that, for the purpose of this activity, the Ace will be one.
5   Allow students to practice finding the Ace by asking the following: 'Show me three'; 'Show me one'; 'Show me four'; 'Show me one'; 'Show me two'; 'Show me one'.
6   Ask students to sort the cards into sets of red and black.
7   Then ask them to put each set in number order, that is, 1 to 5, 1 to 9, or 1 to 10, depending on the numbers you have chosen to use.
8   Ask students to hold up different cards, as you call them out, for example, 'Show me a red 2'.
9   Once you feel they are reasonably comfortable doing this, you can move on to the activity.

Activity

1   Reserve a full set of black and red cards, numbers Ace to 10, for yourself as the caller. You should have a full set of black and red cards in play, ensuring there are nine cards for each student or pair.
2   Shuffle all the cards in play and deal out nine cards to each student or pair.

3   Ask students to put three cards in a row, facing upwards. (Use a 'Bingo Board' for them to put their cards on, if necessary.)
4   Now ask them to make another two rows of three cards, placing them underneath the row they have already made (or to put a card on each box on the Bingo Board).
5   They should now have three rows each of three cards, facing upwards.
6   Shuffle *your* cards and put them in a pile face down.
7   Explain the rules of the game.

To play the game

- Explain that you will turn over a card from your deck and call out what it is, for example, 'black four'.
- Any student who has a black 4 should then turn this card face down.

Continuing the game

- The game continues with the caller turning and calling the cards one at a time and students turning over any card that matches the call.

Winning the game

- The game is won by the first player who has three cards turned over in a row. (Show diagram a on Tutor Sheet 1 on the OHT.)
- The win is checked by the caller asking a student (who is not the winner) to turn over the winner's cards and call out the colour and number of each individual card. The caller checks this against the cards that he or she has turned over from his/her deck.

Extension work

Once students can master this try a second version using row or column (show diagrams a and b on Tutor Sheet 1), and then a third using row, column or diagonal (show Tutor Sheet 1 a, b and c).

Students can then play for a 'Full House', which is when all the cards have been turned over. They either start a new game or continue with the previous game.

There could be prizes for the winner or a chart could be set up to record the number of wins for each student. Keep this chart on the wall and when a student reaches, say, ten points, they then get a reward.

ROW

a

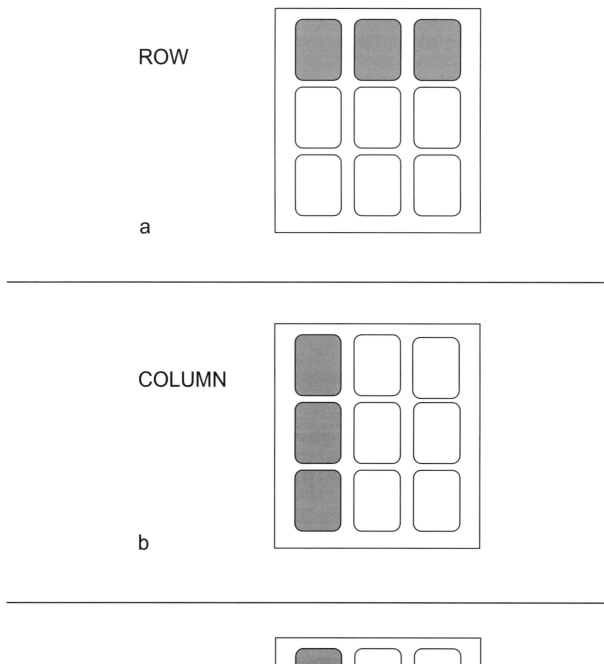

COLUMN

b

DIAGONAL

c

N3 Card Bingo – Tutor Sheet 1
© Nadia Naggar-Smith, *Teaching Foundation Mathematics*, Routledge, 2008

Bingo Board

Lesson N4 – Number lines

Tutor's notes

Number lines are used to assist students with:

- reading, counting and ordering numbers;
- understanding and using spatial language, before and after;
- visualising and memorising the order of written numerals;
- understanding the concepts of more and less; and
- as an introduction to reading off numbers from graduated equipment (e.g. tape measures and measuring jugs).

However, a number line has its limitations in this context in that it neither conceptualises nor demonstrates quantities.

In this lesson, zero has been excluded from the number line, because students are using counting numbers only – if you have nothing you cannot count it. However, students who have reached Milestone 8 and are advancing to the Adult Numeracy core curriculum will need to recognise zero.

Stage 1 item 2 of the lesson requires tutors to show some examples of number lines. A good example of a real number line to use in Stage 1 of the lesson is a paper tape measure (large DIY suppliers are usually very willing to provide students or tutors with these). These tape measures are one metre long and demonstrate the continuation of numbers beyond ten. Students can find the numbers that they are going to be using and cut the tape to the required length.

A ruler is another example of a readily available number line. Mark the ruler to show the numbers in use.

The fact that not all number lines are horizontal can be demonstrated by showing both a measuring jug and an example of a bar chart. (This can be linked to student bar charts from lesson N6.) This lesson uses a horizontal number line, and a vertical number line is used in the 'Measures' part of this book.

Students working with numbers below ten should use the ten length line and only fill in the numbers that they know. They will fill in the other numbers when they become confident with them.

Although zero is not a counting number and can cause confusion when matching counting numbers to quantities and objects, it is used on number lines.

Students should be given the opportunity to make their own selection of a number line for use with the worksheets (tape measures, rulers or their home-made number lines).

The photocopiable tutor's worksheet, which could be enlarged to A3 if necessary, is provided for Activity 1 but you may wish students to create their own lines. The choice is yours. It is advisable to have a few sheets of number stickers at hand for students who find writing challenging.

Use large plastic paper clips as placeholders rather than metal ones for health and safety reasons!

Criteria

Adult Pre-entry Curriculum Framework for Numeracy

Number

Milestone 5 – sub-element 1

Milestone 6 – sub-element 1, sub-element 2 and sub-element 3

Milestone 7 – sub-element 1, sub-element 3, sub-element 4 (sub-element 5 and sub-element 6 with activity 3)

Milestone 8 – sub-element 1, sub-element 2, sub-element 3, sub-element 5b and d, sub-element 6, sub-element 7 and sub-element 8

These elements progress to N1/E1.1, N1/E1.2, N1/E1.3, N1/E1.4, N1/E1.5 in the Adult Numeracy core curriculum.

P scales

Using and applying mathematics　P8

Number　P8

Space, shape and measures　P7

Lesson N4   Number lines

Objectives

To construct a number line and then use it to practice:

*   reading, counting and ordering numbers;
*   spatial language;
*   simple addition and subtraction; and
*   visualising and memorising the order of written numerals.

Resources

*   paper tape measures (one per student) see tutor's notes;
*   rulers (one per student);
*   a calibrated measuring jug;
*   an example of a bar chart;
*   paper or Worksheet 1 (one per student);
*   coloured pens or pencils;
*   sheets of number stickers (in reserve) (see tutor's notes);
*   large paper clips to be used as a pointer or placeholder;
*   Worksheet 1 – one copy for each student;
*   Worksheet 2 – one copy for each student.

Lesson plan

Stage 1: Introduction and class discussion

1   Introduce students to the idea of a number line. Ask if they know what a number line is.
2   Show some examples of number lines, for example, a paper tape measure, a ruler, a measuring jug, a bar chart.
3   Starter questions to ask: 'Have you ever seen one of these before?' 'Do you know what it is?' 'What is it used for?'.
4   Explain that students are going to make their own number line to use throughout the course. Students may work together, but each student will need to have his/her own number line at the end of the activity.
5   Write the numbers they will use for their number line on the board, in the correct order.

Activity 1: Making a number line

1   Give out the materials you have decided to use for the students to: construct the number lines (strips of paper or worksheets, pens, pencils, number stickers).
2   Explain what you want individual students to do. You may want them to: write the numerals in different colours (this helps them with visual memory); use number stickers (for students with poor motor or spatial skills); or create their own stickers.

3   Encourage students to say the numbers out loud as they are constructing their number line, checking their sequence against the numbers on the tape measure or ruler. They may wish to work in pairs. Make the activity as multisensory as you can.

4   Once complete, ask students to show their number lines to the class and read the numbers together.

Activity 2: Using the number line

1   Give the students a paper clip and explain that you want them to place the paper clip on the number you call out.

2   Start by calling the numbers in sequence, allowing time for them to move the paper clip and look at its new position each time. Use commands such as 'Show me one', 'Show me two' and so on, up to ten.

3   Repeat this several times.

4   Now start at ten and move backwards along the line. Repeat this several times.

5   Repeat the 'Show me' commands with random numbers. Do this until students are confident.

6   Invite individual students to choose a number and shout it out, say, for instance, seven.

7   Everyone places their paper clip at 7 and counts to the end of the number line.

Spatial language

1   Invite individual students to show you a number of their choice and to say the name of that number out loud (for example, 'four'). Now ask them which number comes before this one. Repeat this until students are comfortable with finding the number that comes before any given number.

2   Repeat step 1 for numbers that come after a given number.

3   Now select a number and look at both the number that comes before it and the number that comes after it.

4   Repeat step 3.

5   Introduce Worksheet 1 and ask students to use their number lines to fill in the missing numbers.

Activity 3

1   Introduce Worksheet 2, explaining that it shows sections of a number line where some of the numbers are missing.

2   Ask students to use their number line to fill in the missing numbers.

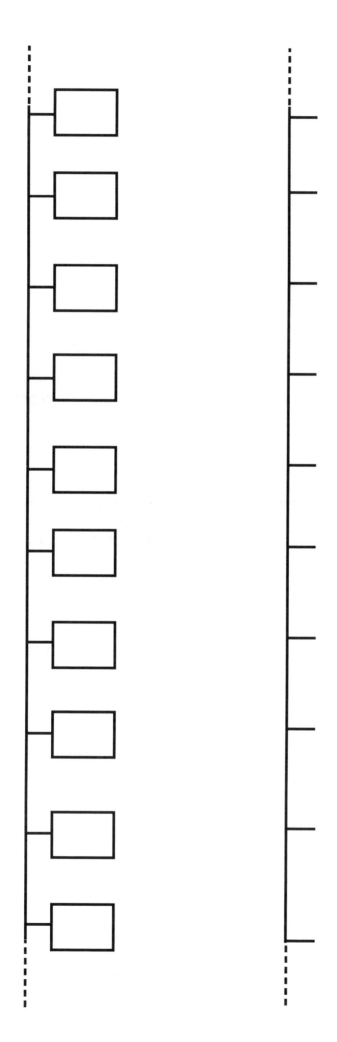

Name:_____ **Date:**_____

Number Lines
Worksheet 1

Fill in the numbers that are BEFORE and AFTER the numbers shown.

1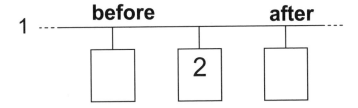

2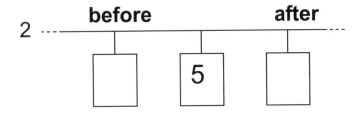

3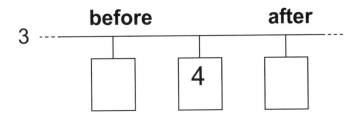

4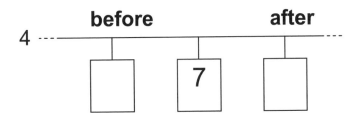

5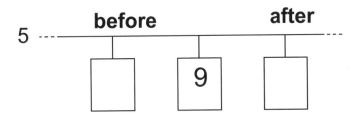

Name:_____ **Date:**_____

Number Lines
Worksheet 2

Fill in the missing numbers on these number lines.

1 | 2 | 3 | | 5 | 6 |

2 | 3 | | 5 | 6 | |

3 | | 6 | | 8 | 9 |

4 | 4 | | | 7 | 8 |

5 | 6 | | | | 10 |

Lesson N5 – Using the number line for addition and subtraction

Tutor's notes

Students will have experienced addition through combining sets and/or partitioning sets but, for problem solving in practical situations, they will also need to be able to count on from a given number. Number lines provide a means of visualising the order and position of numbers and help students to count on and back from a given number. This is a vital tool for problem solving and handling money.

This activity uses number at the connecting stage, working towards holding a number in their head and counting on using their fingers, or by tapping. This is mental mathematics.

Number symbolisation is not used at this stage, as the concept of addition and subtraction is being defined. Symbols are not the concept; they are a shorthand way of writing down all that has gone before. In this lesson, number statements are made in words (written and spoken).

Worksheets 1 (addition and subtraction) are used to record the results of counting one more and one less. Worksheets 2 (addition and subtraction) are used to record the results of finding 1 to 6 more and 1 to 6 less, and may be used as extension work.

After completion of Worksheet 2 (which is about presenting number statements in words), students are then shown how to replace those same words with symbols in Worksheet 3, by revisiting Worksheet 2.

This activity helps students to use their number line to practice counting on from a given number and in recognising and applying the symbols + and = to the process.

Some students may only be able to use the first parts of the worksheets. They should access what they can and keep the worksheet to return to as they progress.

Criteria

Adult Pre-entry Curriculum Framework for Numeracy

Number

Milestone 7 – sub-element 2, sub-element 5, sub-element 6 and sub-element 8
Milestone 8 – sub-element 2, sub-element 5b, c and d, sub-element 7, sub-element 8 and sub-element 10

These elements progress to N1/E1.2, N1/E1.4, N1/E1.5 and N1/E1.6 in the Adult Numeracy core curriculum.

P scales

Using and applying mathematics   P8
Number   P8

Lesson N5   Using the number line for addition and subtraction

Objectives

- to apply counting forward and backward from a given number;
- to read number statements;
- to record results;
- to work towards mental addition and subtraction.

Resources

- Worksheet 1 (Addition) – one copy for each student;
- Worksheet 1 (Subtraction) – one copy for each student;
- Worksheet 2 (Addition) – one copy for each student;
- Worksheet 2 (Subtraction) – one copy for each student;
- number lines.

Lesson plan

Stage 1: Introduction and class discussion

1   Remind students of the number lines lesson by asking them to put their fingers on the number 5 on the number line, and to tell you whether the following numbers come before or after 5: 7, 1, 8, 3, 2, 6 and 9.
Some students (particularly those with spatial directional problems) may need to place cards with 'before' and 'after' written on them in the appropriate position on the line.

2   When students are confident with this, move on to the activity.

Activity

EARLY ADDITION

1   Give out Addition Worksheet 1.
2   Demonstrate the first question, and then ask students to complete the worksheet by recording their answers in the boxes. They should use their number lines.
3   Once students have completed as much of Addition Worksheet 1 as they can, they move on to Addition Worksheet 2 and complete as much as they can.

EARLY SUBTRACTION

1   Before using Subtraction Worksheet 1 (1 less than) students should practice counting backwards along the line.
2   Once students have completed as much of Subtraction Worksheet 1 as they can, they move on to Subtraction Worksheet 2 and complete as much as they can.

Name:_____ Date:_____

Worksheet 1
Addition

Using your number line, complete the following:

1 more than 1 makes ☐

1 more than 2 makes ☐

1 more than 3 makes ☐

1 more than 4 makes ☐

1 more than 5 makes ☐

1 more than 6 makes ☐

1 more than 7 makes ☐

1 more than 8 makes ☐

1 more than 9 makes ☐

Name:_____ **Date:**_____

Worksheet 1
Subtraction

Using your number line, complete the following:

1 less than **2** is [   ]

1 less than **3** is [   ]

1 less than **4** is [   ]

1 less than **5** is [   ]

1 less than **6** is [   ]

1 less than **7** is [   ]

1 less than **8** is [   ]

1 less than **9** is [   ]

Name:_____ Date:_____

Worksheet 2
Addition

Using your number line, complete the following:

2 more than **1** makes ☐

2 more than **3** makes ☐

3 more than **2** makes ☐

3 more than **5** makes ☐

4 more than **2** makes ☐

4 more than **5** makes ☐

5 more than **3** makes ☐

5 more than **4** makes ☐

6 more than **2** makes ☐

3 more than **7** makes ☐

Name:_____ **Date:**_____

<table>
<tr><td>

Worksheet 2
Subtraction
</td></tr>
</table>

Using your number line, complete the following:

1 less than **3** is ☐

2 less than **4** is ☐

2 less than **3** is ☐

3 less than **5** is ☐

4 less than **5** is ☐

4 less than **7** is ☐

3 less than **8** is ☐

5 less than **9** is ☐

Lesson N6 – Introduction to using bar charts

Tutor's notes

Data handling is a problem-solving tool used to help students to see relationships. The skills and concepts of comparing, counting, adding and subtracting (however small the quantities), go hand in hand with organising data in a systematic way. The skill of graphing develops naturally from the student's interest in comparing groups of objects and collecting information. Early sorting and classifying activities enable students to make rough estimates of more and less.

The following list outlines the steps in learning graphing:

Real graphs:
In this type of graph students do not use representation, they compare real objects like shoes, biscuits, cans.

    Step 1:   Comparing two groups
    Step 2:   Comparing three groups

Representation graphs:
These graphs use pictures (2D) or apparatus (3D) like counters, bottle tops, buttons or cubes to stand for real things. It is important to know that students understand what is being represented at this stage.

Histograms may be used if each picture represents only one item.

    Step 1:   Comparing two groups
    Step 2:   Comparing three groups

Real graphs: Comparing four groups
Representation graphs: Comparing four groups
Symbolic graphs: This is the most abstract level of graphing, because symbols are used to represent real things and most are translated back into reality to have meaning. The symbols could be a tally mark or a cross.

This lesson uses representation graphs progressing from two to three sets of information. Counters are used for representation but some students may find bottle tops easier to move around.

You may wish to spread the activities out over several lessons, building on the numbers used or using different themes to reinforce learning.

The introduction and class discussion

The use of drinks for this particular lesson limits the number of different responses. **Tea**, **coffee** and **juice** are sufficient headings for the table, but you can adapt these to suit your students. If students prefer, the headings could be in picture format instead of, or as well as, written words.

You will also need to bring or make some simple examples of bar charts to show students what they will be creating. Students can usually see the information more clearly if the bars on the chart are in squares, rather than one whole block of colour (as shown below).

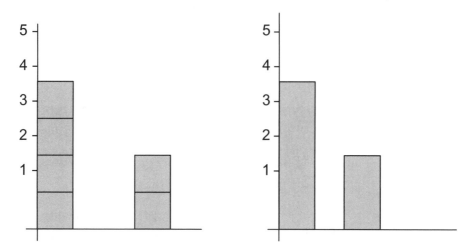

Depending on the ability of the class, you may use blank squared paper or squared paper that has the axis of the bar chart already drawn on. Decide, in advance, whether students will need the number to be written for them, or they will write it themselves. Students may be able to assist each other in writing the numbers on the chart. This will help them in ordering and recalling numbers. Some students may need their number line from their tool kit.

Prepared sticky labels on which students can write tea, coffee and juice and/ or number stickers could prove useful.

Throughout the activity, students should be encouraged to count, to reinforce their application of number concepts.

Criteria

Adult Pre-entry Curriculum Framework for Numeracy

Number

Milestone 6 – sub-element 1, sub-element 2, sub-element 3 and sub-element 4
Milestone 7 – sub-element 1, sub-element 2, sub-element 3 and sub-element 4
Milestone 8 – sub-element 1, sub-element 3, sub-element 4, sub-element 5 and
               sub-element 6

Handling data

Milestone 8 – sub-element 3

These elements progress to N1/E1.1, N1/E1.2, N1/E1.3, HD1/E1.3, HD1/E2.2, HD1/E2.4, HD1/E2.5 in the Adult Numeracy core curriculum.

P scales

Using and applying mathematics   Level 8
Number   Level 8

Lesson N6   Bar charts

Objectives

- to gather information and sort it into groups;
- to record the information;
- to use bar charts to discuss the results.

Resources

- a table, either pre-prepared and laminated, or hand drawn in the lesson (see Tutor's notes);
- different coloured counters, plastic bottle tops or other appropriate objects to be used to represent the drinks;
- squared paper;
- examples of simple bar charts (see tutor's notes).

Lesson plan

Stage 1: Introduction and class discussion

1 Have a discussion about the kind of things everyone had for breakfast and the drinks they had.
2 See which were the most popular and the least popular drinks (by show of hands).

Activity

1 Using either A4 or A3 paper, depending on the number of students you have, either create or give out a Table A and a selection of counters or objects.
2 Ask the students to place counters of one colour for tea, one colour for coffee and another colour for juice in each of the boxes on the top row of the table. This will help them practice their sorting skills.
3 Once the students have done this, ask each student what they had to drink with their breakfast. Everyone can record the responses by moving the appropriate counter or object into the box below. For example, the first student may say he/she had tea for their drink. Everyone will then move one counter as shown below.

N.B. Sometimes students would have had something different, for example, water, chocolate or nothing. If the chart is expanded it becomes too cluttered for students at this level of development. In this case ask them to select one of the items on the chart that they will like everyone to put their counter in.

4 Once all the students have said what they had to drink, they can count the number for each drink. They can write the number on the chart (this makes links between representation and symbolisation) but they must also leave the objects in place.

JUICE	TEA	COFFEE

5 Discuss the chart. Questions to ask: 'Which was the most popular drink?', 'Which was the least popular?'.

6 Show some simple examples of bar charts.

7 Tell the students they are going to create a bar chart to show the drinks they all had at breakfast.

8 Give each student some squared paper to use.

9 Ensure that the squares on the paper are large enough to easily contain the counters or objects students are using for representation.

10 Ask students to put the labels on the x-axis (**Tea**, **Coffee** and **Juice**), if the chart is not already labelled.

11 Now ask students to move the counters or objects they have in, for example, the ¨ea category, on to the squares in the **Tea** column (see diagram below).

12 This should be repeated for each drink.

13 Depending on what you think is most appropriate for your students, the counters or objects could be stuck onto the paper, or they could colour the squares that have a counter or object in them.

14 This activity can be repeated for different information.

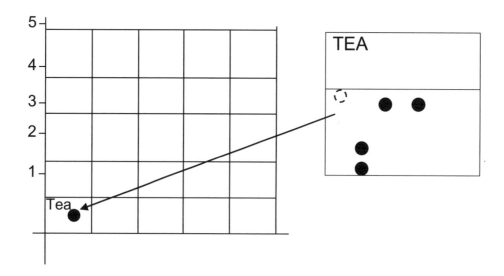

Extension activity

Once students are more familiar with this method, marks or tallies (symbolic representation) could be used instead of counters or objects.

Students could be asked to carry out surveys of their choice in the class, or other appropriate places, and record their results.

Table A

Juice	Tea	Coffee

Lesson N7 – Estimating

Tutor's notes

The ability to estimate is important in the ordinary activities in adult life. There are several aspects of estimation but the aspect used in this lesson may be described as 'realising whether an answer is reasonable'. This grows from early visual comparison of sets of items in terms of 'more' or 'less', to estimating whether the number of items in a set of objects is 'more than', or 'less than' a given number. The final stage uses the language of estimation; 'too high', 'too low' and 'reasonable'.

In this lesson, 'estimation' is explained as 'a guess that is nearly correct'. Cards with 'too high', 'too low' and 'reasonable' written on one side, and 'more', 'less' and 'about right' on the other help students to see links with other mathematics.

Estimating helps students to develop a feel for numbers. It reinforces both the concepts of quantities and number recall. It helps students to make sense of the world around them.

The introductory stages are:

- stage 1: Verbal response only;
- stage 2: Placing labels on a counting strip;
- stage 3: Number lines, rulers or counting strips help students to relate the counting of the objects to the estimates that are 'less than' and those that are 'more than' the exact number. For example, for a set of six objects, 6 is marked on the number line.

1	2	3	4	5	6	7	8	9	10
	Too low				Reasonable			Too high	

Students then point to the first number on the line and say its name, check their number line and say 'too low'; this is repeated until they reach five and then they say 'reasonable', for numbers five, six and seven and continue the count saying 'more than' after each number for as far as you wish. They can check with known language on the back of the cards.

The lesson can be extended to making a sensible guess (estimate) of the number of objects in a set, for example, potatoes in a bag.

Students will need constant reassurance throughout the lesson that they cannot be wrong when they estimate.

Using the worksheets

The worksheets can be used either to combine stage 1 and 2 of the lesson or as a separate activity.

Once students have written their estimate on their worksheet, they should tick their answer before being allowed to count the actual number. This is to make them feel more confident about estimating and to help stop them from wanting to change their estimate once they have made the count.

Criteria

Adult Pre-entry Curriculum Framework for Numeracy

Number

Milestone 6 – sub-element 1, sub-element 2 and sub-element 3
Milestone 7 – sub-element 1, sub-element 2 and sub-element 4
Milestone 8 – sub-element 1, sub-element 3 and sub-element 4

Note: The milestones covered are for the part of the lesson where the students are actually counting.

These elements progress to N1/E1.1, N1/E2.1 in the Adult Numeracy core curriculum.

P scales

Using and applying mathematics   P8
Number   P8

Lesson N7   Estimating

Objectives

- to make simple estimates;
- to reinforce the concept of quantities;
- to practice recall;
- to order numbers;
- to use counting strips.

Resources

- three cards for each student or group with 'too high', 'too low' and 'reasonable' on them. The reverse should have 'more', 'less' and 'about right';
- a small (plastic) bag of potatoes;
- a small (plastic) bag of apples;
- a small (transparent) packet of sweets;
  (There should be between six and ten items in each bag);
- Worksheet 1 – one copy per student;
- Worksheet 2 – one copy per student;
- Worksheet 3 – one copy per student.

Lesson plan

Stage 1: Introduction and class discussion

1 Have a discussion on the difference between an estimate and a guess. Students may be familiar with some situations where an estimate will be used, such as builders' estimates, estimating the amount of paint needed to decorate a room, and so on.
2 Talk about the language of estimation, linking it to known language: 'When an estimate is too much, we say it is too high'; 'When it is too little, we say it is too low'; 'When it is not quite, but nearly, right, we say it is reasonable'; 'When it is exact, we say spot on'.

Activity 1

1 Students can work alone or in pairs for this activity.
2 Give out three cards to each student or group, with 'too low', 'too high' and 'reasonable' written on them.
3 Put some objects into a bag, for example, six apples, and tell the students you are going to estimate the number of apples in the bowl and they must decide whether the number you have said is 'too low', 'too high' or 'reasonable'.
4 You could then say, 'If I said there are 100 apples in the bag, do you think my estimate is "too high", "too low" or "reasonable?".' Hold each card up as you say this to familiarise students with the cards. Students should then hold up the card that they think is correct – in this case, the one that says 'too high'.
5 Call out other numbers getting closer to the actual number each time.
6 Now count the apples and ask students to mark the exact number on their counting strip.
7 Once they have established a 'reasonable' answer discuss what you think other reasonable answers might be.

Activity 2

1 Give out Worksheet 1 and explain to your students that they are going to write down what they did to help them to remember.
2 Work through the worksheet step by step.

Activity 3

1 Follow steps 1 to 7 of Activity 1.
2 Give out Worksheet 2 and assist your students to fill it in.

Activity 4

1 Follow steps 1 to 7 of Activity 1.
2 Give out Worksheet 3 and assist your students to fill it in.

Once the students are familiar with recording on their sheets, you can then give them handouts with other items on, such as shapes or animals, and ask them to complete the worksheets as before.

Name:_____ **Date:**_____

Estimating
Worksheet 1

This is what we did

1	2	3	4	5	6	7	8	9	10

Put a cross on your estimate.

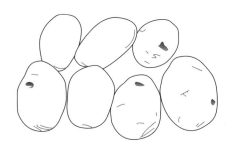

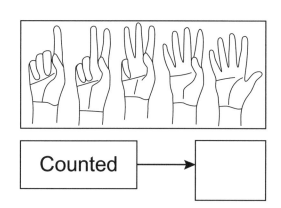

My estimate was

'too high'

'too low'

'reasonable'

© Nadia Naggar-Smith, *Teaching Foundation Mathematics*, Routledge, 2008

Name:_____ **Date:**_____

Estimating
Worksheet 2

This is what we did

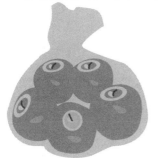

Looked

Estimated

1	2	3	4	5	6	7	8	9	10

Put a cross on your estimate.

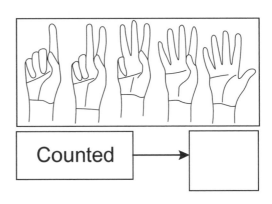

Counted	→	

My estimate was

too high

too low

reasonable

Name:_____ **Date:**_____

Estimating
Worksheet 3

This is what we did

Looked

Estimated

1	2	3	4	5	6	7	8	9	10

Put a cross on your estimate.

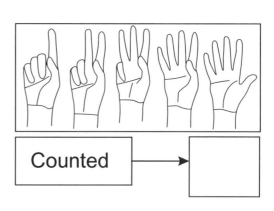

Counted	→	

My estimate was

'too high'

'too low'

'reasonable'

Lesson N8 – Early multiplication

Tutor's notes

Multiplication grows out of an ability to see number patterns and to use equal addition. This lesson helps to develop learning opportunities in both of these areas of number work.

The lesson sets learning opportunities for students to experience counting in twos (eyes and hands) and working with pairs (gloves and socks). The introduction to the lesson presents life experience (physical experience) discussion and representation with 3D objects (e.g. counters or bottle tops). The activities are worksheet-generated discussion (2D representation) and recording.

The worksheets have been prepared so that they require the minimum amount of artwork from the students. If you have time it is better to allow students to do their own artwork, as personalisation strengthens concepts, but be prepared for time differences in completion of the worksheets, because some students will add a great amount of detail.

The extension work builds on the language used at the end of Activity 1, that is, pairs. After a short demonstration, students are expected to work in pairs to fill the sheets unaided. The final worksheet is only for students who have completed all the previous activities.

At each stage of this lesson you may need to extend the time spent at that particular level by making further similar worksheets.

Criteria

Adult Pre-entry Curriculum Framework for Numeracy

Number

Milestone 7 – sub-element 1, sub-element 2, sub-element 4, sub-element 5 and
sub-element 8a
Milestone 8 – sub-element 1, sub-element 3, sub-element 5, sub-element 6,
sub-element 7 and sub-element 10c

These elements progress to N1/E1.1, N1/E1.2 and N1/E1.4 in the Adult Numeracy core curriculum.

P scales

Using and applying   P8
Number   P8

Lesson N8   Early multiplicaton

Objectives

- to develop an ability to see patterns;
- to count in twos, with the help of a number line;
- to apply counting and comparison skills to multiplication.

Resources

- a selection of objects, enough for ten per student;
- a number line or ruler for each pair of students;
- Worksheets 1, 2, 3 and 4 for each student;
- two pairs of gloves;
- two pairs of socks;
- stickers of students if needed for extension activity (optional).

Lesson plan

Stage 1: Introduction and class discussion

1 Pose the question, 'How many eyes do three students have between them?'. Allow them to solve the problem by themselves.
2 Ask students to show you the answer, either with apparatus or by writing it down.
3 Try two or three other numbers and see if they can figure out the totals.

Activity

1 Students may work in pairs.
2 Give out Worksheet 1.
3 Ask students to fill in the eyes on the smiley faces. Each time they finish a row they must write the numbers in the box.
4 As a group, read the worksheets: 'One person has two eyes', 'Two people have four eyes'. Continue this, in order, to the end of the worksheet.
5 Questions to ask: 'Two people, how many eyes altogether?' 'One person, how many eyes?' Continue asking questions like this until the students understand how to find the answers.
6 Ask students to find the number line at the bottom of the worksheet and circle (put a ring around) all the numbers in the boxes in the 'eyes' boxes. You will need to demonstrate this.
7 Hand out Worksheet 2, 'Hands', and complete it the same way as Worksheet 1. Some pairs of students may be able to do this unassisted.

Extension work

PAIRS OF STUDENTS

1 Students work in pairs for this activity to develop discussion. Draw their attention to the fact that they are working in pairs; ask them how many are there in a pair, and how many are there in two pairs.

2   Hand out Worksheet 3, 'Pairs of students', and remind them how they filled the 'Eyes' worksheet. They should be able to work together to fill in the worksheet.

3   If students are not comfortable drawing, they could write names of students they know, in pairs, and then count the number of names. Alternatively, they could use stickers with pictures of people, or make a mark for each student.

PAIRS OF GLOVES

1   Hold up a glove and ask who can tell you what it is.

2   Hold up two gloves and ask: 'How many gloves am I holding up now?' They will probably say two. Try to lead them into saying 'a pair' before you tell them that two gloves make a pair.

3   Hand out Worksheet 4. Make the students complete Worksheet 4.

4   Worksheets 5a–e are only for students who have completed all the previous activities. You should select the appropriate worksheet(s) from 5a to 5e, depending on individual students.

Name:_____ **Date:**_____

How Many Eyes?

1 person ☺ ☐ eyes

2 people ☺ ☺ ☐ eyes

3 people ☺ ☺ ☺ ☐ eyes

4 people ☺ ☺ ☺ ☺ ☐ eyes

5 people ☺ ☺ ☺ ☺ ☺ ☐ eyes

1 2 3 4 5 6 7 8 9 10

Name:_____ **Date:**_____

How Many Hands?

1 person [ ] hands

2 people [ ] hands

3 people [ ] hands

4 people [ ] hands

5 people [ ] hands

1   2   3   4   5   6   7   8   9   10

Name:_____ **Date:**_____

How Many Students?

1 pair
of students

☐ = ☐ students

A pair of students

2 pairs
of students

☐ ☐ = ☐ students

3 pairs
of students

☐ ☐ ☐ = ☐ students

4 pairs
of students

☐ ☐ ☐ ☐ = ☐ students

5 pairs
of students

☐ ☐ ☐ ☐ ☐ = ☐ students

1 2 3 4 5 6 7 8 9 10

N8 Early Multiplication – Worksheet 3 (Pairs of students)
© Nadia Naggar-Smith, *Teaching Foundation Mathematics*, Routledge, 2008

Name:_____ **Date:**_____

How Many Gloves?

1 person   □ = □ gloves

A pair of gloves

2 people   □ □ = □ gloves

3 people   □ □ □ = □ gloves

4 people   □ □ □ □ = □ gloves

5 people   □ □ □ □ □ = □ gloves

1   2   3   4   5   6   7   8   9   10

N8 Early Multiplication – Worksheet 4 (Gloves)
© Nadia Naggar-Smith, *Teaching Foundation Mathematics*, Routledge, 2008

Worksheet 5a

and ○ ○ □   makes   ○ ○ ○ ○ ○ ○ ○ ○ ○ ○ ○ □

and ○ ○ □   and ○ ○ □   makes   ○ ○ ○ ○ ○ ○ ○ ○ ○ □

and ○ ○ □   and ○ ○ □   and ○ ○ □   makes   ○ ○ ○ ○ ○ ○ ○ ○ ○ ○ ○ □

and ○ ○ □   and ○ ○ □   and ○ ○ □   and ○ ○ □   makes   ○ ○ ○ ○ ○ ○ ○ ○ ○ ○ ○ ○ ○ ○ □

N8 Early Multiplication – Worksheet 5a
© Nadia Naggar-Smith, *Teaching Foundation Mathematics*, Routledge, 2008

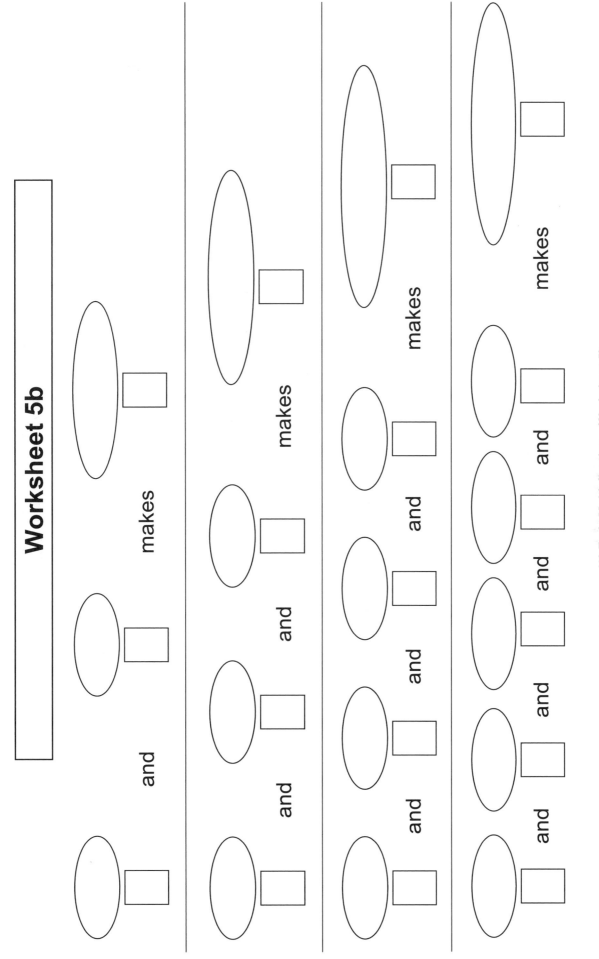

Worksheet 5b

⬭ and ⬭ makes ⬭

⬭ and ⬭ makes ⬭

⬭ and ⬭ and ⬭ makes ⬭

⬭ and ⬭ and ⬭ and ⬭ makes ⬭

N8 Early Multiplication – Worksheet 5b
© Nadia Naggar-Smith, *Teaching Foundation Mathematics*, Routledge, 2008

Worksheet 5c

☐ and ☐ makes ☐

☐ and ☐ makes ☐

☐ and ☐ makes ☐

☐ and ☐ and ☐ makes ☐

N8 Early Multiplication – Worksheet 5c

© Nadia Naggar-Smith, *Teaching Foundation Mathematics*, Routledge, 2008

Name:_____ **Date:**_____

Worksheet 5d

☐ lot of 2 makes ☐

☐ lots of 2 make ☐

☐ lots of 2 make ☐

☐ lots of 2 make ☐

☐ lots of 2 make ☐

Name:_____ **Date:**_____

☐ lot of **2** = ☐

☐ lots of **2** = ☐

☐ lots of **2** = ☐

☐ lots of **2** = ☐

☐ lots of **2** = ☐

Lesson N9 – Addition and subtraction strips

Tutor's notes

This lesson connects the concepts of addition, subtraction and equals to their symbols. In preparation for the lesson students make their own counting strips using the numbers 1 to 9. They can use the numbers in any order and repeat them as often as they want. Vertical number strips are easier for students to both read and hold their place, by using their thumb or folding the strip. They may write their names on the back of the strip.

There are several ways to make these strips for this activity. Some suggestions are:

- use the paper strips as they are presented at the end of this lesson;
- photocopy the strips onto card and laminate them. Students could then write numbers in the squares, using drywipe pens and the strips could be reused;
- attach pieces of Velcro to both the strips and the individual numbers. These can also be reused.

Choose whatever is the most appropriate for your students and the resources available.

All the items to be counted should be of the same type of object; for example, plastic bottle tops. Plastic bottle tops can be collected by the students. They are readily available everyday items and are easy for students to pick up and move around. Using similar objects helps students to focus on the whole group, rather than the individual items within that group. This stimulates visualisation of quantities when increasing and decreasing the overall size of the group. Use about twenty objects.

For the activities students work in threes: the 'reader', the 'doer' and the 'recorder',

- the 'reader' is the person who will read out the numbers from the strips;
- the 'doer' is the person who will physically add or remove the given number of bottle tops (or other objects used);
- the 'recorder' is the person who will write down the sums.

Students should swap roles after three sums have been completed. The strips should be exchanged between the groups throughout the lesson.

The introduction to the lesson involves making the strips and clarifying their use. It also introduces the symbols of addition, subtraction and equals.

This first linking of concepts to symbols is paramount to future understanding of symbolic mathematics in everyday life. It is important to connect the symbols to the language of the students, for example, 'and' or 'add', 'take away' and 'makes' or 'altogether'. To use correct terminology, after the concept/symbol links have been established, is part of the Basic Mathematics curriculum.

Activity 1 is a small step activity, leading into the main activity. It introduces students to recording what they did by selecting the correct symbols, without recording their answers. It provokes the students to see the need for an answer and, thus, progress to Activity 2. However, some students may need to stay with this activity for a long time and you may need to regroup your students, in order to promote individual progress.

Activity 2 requires students to record both numbers and process symbols. If Activity 1 has been mastered, then this activity should run smoothly. If not, students may need to repeat Activity 1.

Worksheet 2 has been designed for all three students in the group to fill in their own section of the worksheet.

Criteria

Adult Pre-entry Curriculum Framework for Numeracy

Number

Milestone 5 – sub-element 1
Milestone 6 – sub-element 1, sub-element 2 and sub-element 3
Milestone 7 – sub-element 1, sub-element 3, sub-element 4
Milestone 8 – sub-element 1, sub-element 2, sub-element 3, sub-element 5b and d,
              sub-element 6, sub-element 7 and sub-element 8

These elements progress to N1/E1.1, N1/E1.2, N1/E1.3, N1/E1.4, N1/E1.5 in the Adult Numeracy core curriculum.

P scales

Number   P8

Lesson N9   Addition and subtraction strips

Objectives

- to link concepts to symbols;
- to visualise increasing and decreasing of quantities;
- to compare;
- to solve problems;
- to record.

Resources

- a number strip, made by the students, with the numbers 1–5 or 1–10 (see tutor's notes);
- about twenty bottle tops (or other like objects – see tutor's notes) per group of three students;
- Worksheet 1 – one for each group;
- Worksheet 2 – one for each group;
- a ruler or number line, if appropriate.

Lesson plan

Stage 1: Introduction and class discussion

For the practical activity in this lesson, students move down their number strips, one number at a time. As each number is read by the 'reader', the 'doer' changes the quantity of the objects to reflect the number being read. At each step the 'reader', the 'doer' and the 'recorder' should all say how many objects they must add or subtract in order to move from number to number.

1   The lesson begins with tutors instructing their students on how to make the number strips (see tutor's notes).
2   Each student makes his or her own number strip.
3   Tutors demonstrate to students how they will be expected to work with their number strips.
4   Invite a student to be the 'reader' and to read, out loud, the first number on their strip. Then invite a 'recorder' to write that number on the board (for example, 5) as a starter number.
5   Invite a student to be the 'doer' and place that number of objects on the table at the front of the room.
6   Explain that as the 'reader' reads down the list of numbers from the start, the 'doer' will need to change the number of objects to match the new number. Sometimes the 'doer' will need to add some more and sometimes the 'doer' will need to take some away.
7   Ask the 'reader' to call out the next number on their strip (say 6).
8   Ask the class 'If you have five (pointing to both the number 5 and the group of five items) and you need six; do you need some **more** [bottle tops] to make six, or do you need to **take some** [bottle tops] **away** to make six?'

This amount of detail is necessary, and the language should not be varied until students have the confidence to work in groups of three, at the same task.

As students become confident with this 'saying' and 'doing' activity, they move on to Activity 1.

Activity 1

1   Set up the activity by dividing students into groups of three – one 'reader', one 'doer' and one 'recorder'.
2   The 'reader' selects a number strip. The 'doer' collects the apparatus (twenty items). The 'recorder' is given a copy of Worksheet 1, a record sheet.
3   Remind students of the + and − signs on the record sheet and draw their attention to the last box. This box is there to record the number of times that two consecutive numbers occur. For example, if the 'reader' calls out 'four' and then the next number they call out is also 'four', then they will do 'nothing', as the number remains the same and they need not add or take away any bottle tops.
4   Students complete the activity recording their movements on the record sheet. They then count the number of ticks in each column and record the number in the dedicated boxes.
5   Students talk about their results.

Activity 2

1   Give each group of three a copy of Worksheet 2.
2   Explain that they are now going to make some sums by counting how many objects they have taken away or added to make the new number. Demonstrate how you expect them to complete this task.
3   They will need to do this activity, without any recording, until they are confident enough to write something down.
4   Repeat the activity and fill in the worksheet.

N9 Addition and Subtraction Strips
© Nadia Naggar-Smith, *Teaching Foundation Mathematics*, Routledge, 2008

Name:_____ **Date:**_____

Tick the box, to show what you did to make the number.

add +	take away –	nothing

Name: _____

Date: _____

1st number	+ or –	2nd number	=	Answer
?	+/–	?		?
			=	
			=	
			=	

Lesson N10 – Connecting concepts to symbols (addition and equals)

Tutor's notes

This activity offers opportunities for students to rehearse and reinforce their counting, sorting and early addition skills. It encourages discussion and logical reasoning at all stages, using mathematical language to discuss what does and does not belong in the subsets. These are important problem-solving techniques.

Throughout this section of the book, attention has been drawn to the fact that the mature learner has often met symbols without understanding where and when to use them. Although the P scales assessment criteria do not specifically mention addition and equals signs, the Adult Pre-entry Curriculum Framework does. It is important to connect the concept to its symbol before advancing to Basic Maths, and this lesson is an example of the linking of concepts to their symbols. It is the stepping stone that links Foundation Maths to Basic Maths.

The lesson progresses through four stages of developing mathematical reasoning (mentioned in the introduction to this book). These are:

1   physical experience;
2   language to describe that experience;
3   representation;
4   recording using symbols.

The pace of the lesson must always be determined by the students; not moving too quickly, whilst still challenging each student. You may choose to spread the lesson over several maths sessions, or even use it as a topic.

Stage 1

The first part of the lesson uses five students to demonstrate addition by partitioning sets.

The partitioning of the universal set of five students into two subsets, for example three and two, is discussed by the group. Nothing is written down at this stage. The established concept is being revised and sharpened, before another mathematics building block is added.

Students are required to link the correct numerals to the number of students in each subset. This is familiar to them and should make them feel comfortable with the task. When they are comfortable, they are asked if they know the sign for 'and', and guided into accepting + (plus) as the answer. The card bearing that symbol is placed between the two groups of students. The symbols 2+3 are first read aloud, in unison, and then recorded on the board, thus using auditory, visual and tactile sensory learning.

Students are then asked to count how many students are there altogether.

A similar schematic approach is taken (in both teaching and learning) to introduce the sign for altogether (= equals).

The linking is made through small steps and can be extended to partitioning a group of ten students, if necessary.

The activities

Students move through the activities to one step beyond their comfort zone; some will be able to reach, and complete, the extension work while others may not.

The worksheet showing ten faces can:

- be left intact for students who prefer a 2D approach;
- be cut into separate cards for students who prefer a more tactile approach;
- be used as a five card activity, in which case use only one column of faces;
- be used as a ten card activity, using either all ten cards from the onset of the activity, or progressing from five to ten cards.

The worksheets guide students through the process of recording from using words, to recording using mathematics symbols. They should be encouraged to read the number statements aloud at each stage of the process. This maximises the number of senses being used at any given time.

Extension work is provided for students who are ready to expand the concept. This activity applies their knowledge and understanding to a different aspect of mathematics (shapes).

Criteria

Adult Pre-entry Curriculum Framework for Numeracy

Number

Milestone 6 – sub-element 3
Milestone 7 – sub-element 2, sub-element 4, sub-element 5 and sub-element 8
Milestone 8 – sub-element 3, sub-element 5, sub-element 6, sub-element 7 and
               sub-element 10

P scales

Using and applying mathematics   P7
                                  P8
Number   P8

Lesson N10   Connecting concepts to symbols (addition and equals)

Objectives

- to connect concepts to symbols (+ and =);
- to rehearse counting skills;
- to rehearse sorting skills;
- to rehearse addition by partitioning;
- to apply mathematical language to symbols;
- to use logic and reasoning;
- to use discussion and decision making.

Resources

- A4 cards with the numbers 1 to 10 on them;
- one A4 card with a + sign on it;
- one A4 card with an = sign on it;
- a coloured OHT of Worksheet 1a, 'People';
- a copy of Worksheet 1a, 'People', per student. (Note that for students who are going to cut this sheet into cards, you may need to photocopy it onto light card.);
- copies of 'People (up to 5)' and 'People (up to 10)' as appropriate.

Extension work

- one copy of 'Shapes' per student;
- copies of Worksheets 1 and 2a or 2b (one set per student).

Lesson plan

Stage 1: Introduction and class discussion

1 Draw the class or group together and explain that today they are going to start the lesson by looking for things that are the same and some that are not the same. (Avoid using the word different.)

2 Give requests like: 'If you are wearing jeans, stand up', and wait until all the students who are wearing jeans are standing up. Now, ask if any of the students sitting down are wearing jeans. So we can say, 'Those people are wearing jeans' (pointing to the group at the front of the room), and 'All of those people are not wearing jeans' (pointing to the students who are sitting down). You may need to repeat this several times because a negative-logic question takes longer to assimilate.

3 Continue to ask similar questions until students are comfortable with the logical language involved. Requests could include trainers, T-shirts, socks or buttons.

4 This activity should be repeated using questions about physical characteristics, for example, short hair, brown eyes, dimples and so on, until students are familiar with identifying different characteristics.

Activity 1

This activity is a whole class or group activity and should be used first with groups of five students and then extended to ten.

1 Ask a group of five students to come out to the front.
2 Now explain that everyone is going to help to sort a group of five volunteers into two different groups and that they will see different ways of dividing the group of five (partitioning).
3 Count the number of students in the group and emphasise that there are five of them.
4 Ask, for example, 'How many people are wearing jeans in this group?'.
5 Allow the class to identify who is wearing jeans and then ask those students wearing jeans to move to one side and count them again. Ask one of the students in this group to hold up the A4 card with the number that shows how many students have jeans on, for example '3'.
6 Invite a volunteer to write that number [3] on the board.
7 Using the same group, ask, 'How many people are **not** wearing jeans in this group?'.
8 Ask one of the students to hold up a card with that number. In this example it will be '2'.
9 Invite a volunteer to write that number [2] on the board.
10 Talk about the numbers on the board making them into a number sentence. 'How many students were wearing jeans? [3], and how many students were not wearing jeans? [2]'
11 Write and read, 'That is 3 and 2'.
12 Ask if anyone knows the sign for 'and'. Then ask them to find the '+' (plus) sign and stand between the 2 groups holding up the '+' (plus) sign.
13 Read the people sum: '3 and 2'.
14 The group then reads the sum on the board '3 [students] and 2 [students]'.
15 Invite a volunteer to replace the word 'and' with the plus sign on the board. Read '3 + 2'.
16 Repeat this activity using different clothing or characteristics.

You may need to take a lesson break here.

Activity 2

1 Add another number building block by repeating some of the previous tasks and say, for example, '3 and 2, how many people altogether?', count them and say '3 and 2 make 5'.
2 When students recognise the answer is always five, repeat steps 12 to 16 with the equals sign (makes) (altogether).
3 Students may write down these sums, if appropriate.

Activity 3

This activity moves to pictorial representation. Some students will prefer the pictures on the worksheet to be made into individual cards so that they can move them into sets (see tutor's notes).

1 Give each student either Worksheet 1 (Faces), or cards.
2 Show the same sheet of ten faces on the OHP, white board, or just hold it up for the students to see.
3 Start by using five faces (show only one column).
4 Ask how many faces there are.
5 Now ask how many of the faces are smiling, then how many are not smiling and how many faces there are altogether (do not record them at this stage).
6 Repeat step 5 with different characteristics.

7   Use all ten faces (if appropriate) and repeat five.
8   Hand out either Worksheet 2 (Faces up to 5) or Worksheet 3 (Faces up to 10) and assist students to complete the number stories.

Extension work

This activity applies linking concepts to symbols to another aspect of mathematics, i.e., shapes.

1   Show Worksheet 4a – 'Shapes' – and talk about the different shapes: how many sides they have and their colour.
2   Then give out Worksheet 4b 'Shapes' and show students how to complete it, by forming the sums.

Name:_____ **Date:**_____

Worksheet 2
Faces (up to 5)

---

1 How many people are smiling? ☐

+

2 How many people are **not smiling**? ☐

=

3 How many people are there altogether? ☐

4 Write the sum ☐ + ☐ = ☐

---

1 How many people are wearing glasses? ☐

+

2 How many people are **not wearing glasses**? ☐

=

3 How many people are there altogether? ☐

4 Write the sum ☐ + ☐ = ☐

---

1 How many people have hair? ☐

\+

2 How many people do **not have hair**? ☐

\=

3 How many people are there altogether? ☐

4 Write the sum   ☐ + ☐ = ☐

---

1 How many people are wearing a hat? ☐

\+

2 How many people are **not wearing a hat**? ☐

\=

3 How many people are there altogether? ☐

4 Write the sum   ☐ + ☐ = ☐

Name:_____ **Date:**_____

Worksheet 3
Faces (up to 10)

1 How many people are smiling? ☐

+

2 How many people are **not smiling**? ☐

=

3 How many people are there altogether? ☐

4 Write the sum   ☐ + ☐ = ☐

---

1 How many people are on the phone? ☐

+

2 How many people are **not on the phone**? ☐

=

3 How many people are there altogether? ☐

4 Write the sum   ☐ + ☐ = ☐

1 How many people are winking?

□

+

2 How many people are **not winking**?

□

=

3 How many people are there altogether?

□

4 Write the sum   □ + □ = □

---

1 How many people are wearing a hat?

□

+

2 How many people are **not wearing a hat**?

□

=

3 How many people are there altogether?

□

4 Write the sum   □ + □ = □

1 How many people are wearing glasses? ☐

+

2 How many people are **not wearing glasses**? ☐

=

3 How many people are there altogether? ☐

4 Write the sum   ☐ + ☐ = ☐

---

1 How many people have hair? ☐

+

2 How many people do **not have hair**? ☐

=

3 How many people are there altogether? ☐

4 Write the sum   ☐ + ☐ = ☐

Name:_____ **Date:**_____

Shapes

---

1 How many shapes have 4 sides? ☐

  +

2 How many shapes **do not have 4 sides**? ☐

  =

3 How many shapes are there altogether? ☐

4 Write the sum ☐ + ☐ = ☐

---

5 How many shapes are round? ☐

  +

6 How many shapes are **not round**? ☐

  =

7 How many shapes are there altogether? ☐

8 Write the sum ☐ + ☐ = ☐

9 How many shapes are yellow?   □

                                      +

10 How many shapes are **not yellow**?   □

                                      =

11 How many shapes are there altogether?   □

12 Write the sum   □ + □ = □

_____

13 How many shapes are red?   □

                                      +

14 How many shapes are **not red**?   □

                                      =

15 How many shapes are there altogether?   □

16 Write the sum   □ + □ = □

Part II
Measure

Introduction to Measure

Measurement provides a 'natural way' into the development of number concepts, handling data and life skills.

Although students would have heard the names of standard measurements, for example, litres, metres and kilograms, these are not used at the pre-entry level, or in the P scales. At this level of development, the aim is to help students understand the process of measurement and to compare a variety of real things. The focus is on understanding the 'whole' and the numbers and names focus the student's attention on a 'particular' difference.

Standard measures, therefore, should be put to one side and re-introduced when students have had an opportunity to create their own arbitrary measures and fully explore the idea of measurement. The aim is to assist them to understand the process of measurement and not just to compare numbers.

What do we measure?

We measure time, weight, length, capacity, area, angles, speed, volume and density.

Lessons in this section of the book present opportunities for students to strengthen and clarify concepts of time, weight, length, capacity and money.

The lessons on time involve the life skills of sequencing daily events; reading, writing and ordering days of the week; recognising months of the year; using a calendar and a timetable.

In preparation for handling money when shopping, recognition of coins is revised and enhanced by using a multisensory approach to help students to recognise coins in reality situations, that is, feeling for them in a pocket or a purse.

A second lesson on using coins is presented as a game. The game applies the skill of adding one and subtracting one to using money. There are differentiated worksheets promoting recording of results.

The early measurement of length aims to enrich both the concept of 'between-ness' and the ability to estimate. The lesson on weight helps students to clear misconceptions between 'big' and 'heavy'. The lesson on capacity compares the capacity of drink containers and uses appropriate mathematics language to describe them, for example, 'holds more than', 'holds less than', 'holds the same amount as'.

Practice in measurement is linked with practice of estimation and handling data. Simple recording sheets are provided for both these areas of mathematics. Ability to sort items into sets is extended through measures.

Number Tool Kit

The number tools required for measurement at this stage of development are:

- counting (to ten and beyond);
- ordering number (to five or ten or beyond);
- reading and writing numerals (to 10);
- early concepts of addition (more than);
- early concepts of subtraction (less than);
- early concepts of 'equals' (the same as);
- the use of a number line (to five or ten); and
- estimating.

How do we measure?

There are four stages of development of measurement: comparison, ordering, arbitrary measures and measuring scales.

Comparison of two items

Here, items are compared for similarities and differences.

Practice in comparing lengths, capacity and weights enables students to develop concepts and language of 'more than', 'less than', 'the same as', 'shorter', 'longer', 'heavier', 'lighter' and 'fuller'.

Ordering (more than two)

Practice in ordering lengths, capacity and weights enables students to develop concepts and language of:

- long/longer/longest;
- short/shorter/shortest;
- heavy/heavier/heaviest;
- full/fuller/fullest;
- the same weight as/the same length as/the same number as.

Arbitrary (non-standard measures)

The use of non-standard units of measurement, such as 'handspans' and 'cupfuls', leads to an understanding of the basic concept of 'between-ness'.

If a cupboard measures more than eight 'handspans' but less than nine 'handspans', then a true answer to the question, 'How wide is the cupboard?' is 'It is between eight and nine handspans'. This is often used in telling the time and is the beginning of seeing the need to subdivide whole units.

Measuring scales

Although measuring scales are not used at this stage in the curriculum, unnumbered calibrations are used to keep count of the number of units of liquid that have been poured into a container. This links calibration to the number line used in the number section of the book.

The lessons in this section of the book encourage students to link estimation and measurement. This helps to develop both visualisation of measurement and the need to give a sensible answer.

Lesson M1 – Length: footprints and handspans

Tutor's notes

The concepts of length in the Adult Pre-entry Curriculum Framework are developed through language and application of number. In this lesson, the language emphasised is:

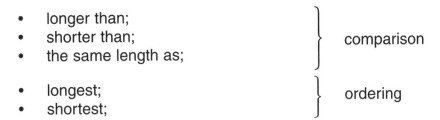

- longer than;
- shorter than;   } comparison
- the same length as;

- longest;   } ordering
- shortest;

and from the Number Tool Kit:

- how many;
- between;

- too high;
- too low;   } estimation
- reasonable.

The objective of the lesson is to make sense of mathematical language that is already in use and to provide the vocabulary for the discussion of comparisons.

Students should be encouraged to estimate their answer, before measuring the items. It is important that you explain to them that they cannot be wrong when they estimate, as students will often be anxious about getting their answer 'right'. Using the expression 'Not quite, but nearly right' will reduce the anxiety many students have about 'exact answers'.

For Activity 4, students will need to cut out their 'handspan'. Many students may not have the fine motor skills needed to cut around the fingers on the drawing of their hand-span and often have difficulty deciding which finger to measure to or from. To help overcome this problem, students should draw around their thumb, and little finger, grouping their three middle fingers together.

Introducing arbitrary units of length that are personal to the students, such as 'my foot-print' or 'my handspan', takes learning far beyond the realm of the classroom. These measures are with the students anywhere, anytime, and students should be encouraged to use them outside the classroom.

Students should be encouraged to cut out several copies (at least two) of their footprints, or handspans, before using them for measuring, as it will be easier for them to count the number used.

Criteria

Adult Pre-entry Curriculum Framework for Numeracy

Measure, shape and space: common measures

Milestone 4 – sub-element 1
Milestone 5 – sub-element 1b
Milestone 6 – sub-element 1b
Milestone 7 – sub-element 4 and sub-element 7
Milestone 8 – sub-element 2 and sub-element 3

P scales

Space, shape and measures   P8
Using and applying mathematics   P8

Lesson M1   Footprints and handspans

Objectives

- to practice language used when comparing length;
- to develop concepts of the need for standardised measure;
- to apply estimation;
- to record results.

Resources

- paper or card to make 'footprints' and 'handspans';
- broad tip felt pens;
- pens and pencils;
- scissors;
- Worksheet – Footprints (1a) – one per student;
- Worksheet – Footprints (1b) – one per student;
- Worksheet – Handspans (2a) – one per student;
- Worksheet – Handspans (2b) – one per student.

Lesson plan

Stage 1: Introduction and class discussion

1 Have a discussion about different shoe sizes in the class. Compare to see who they think has the largest and smallest feet.
2 Ask the students to draw around their foot on a piece of paper or card, and then cut out their footprint. They should write their name on their footprint.
3 Now ask students to see if they can find someone else with the same size footprint.
4 Ask students to put the footprints in order from largest to smallest (longest to shortest) and make a note on the board of the names, in order. Ask questions like, 'Which footprint is longer/shorter?' 'Which footprints are of the same size?'.

Activity 1

1 Students may work in pairs or small groups for the first activity.
2 In pairs or groups ask students to compare footprints and see who has the longest footprint in their group.

Stage 2: Introduction and class discussion

1 Demonstrate how footprints could be used as a unit of measure.
2 Explain and discuss the idea that some of the items will not be an exact number of footprints. Choose an object in the classroom that is not an exact number of footprints and explain that we will describe this as, for example, 'more than three footprints and less than four footprints long. We will say, "It is **between** three and four footprints long."'

3   Practice this with students, until they are comfortable using these expressions.

Activity 2

1   Choose a suitable object in the classroom and ask students to *estimate*, then find out how many of the longest footprints it takes to measure the item. For example, the width of the corridor.
    Record the result of the measurement.
2   Explain that they are now going to measure the same item using the shortest footprint in their group.
3   Discuss whether they think they will need more or less footprints.
4   Students measure the object and record their answer.
5   Discuss why they used more footprints when they used the shorter one.

Activity 3

1   Explain the 'Footprints 1a' worksheet and ask students to complete it, using their own footprints, and record their answers on the worksheet.
2   Show students how to complete Worksheet 'Footprints 1b' and ask them to complete it.

Activity 4

1   Make some 'handspan' measures (see tutor's notes).
2   Explain the 'Handspans' worksheet and ask students to complete it, using their own handspans, and record their answers on the worksheet.

Name:_____ Date:_____

Footprints (1a)

Use your footprint to find the following:

1 How many of your footprints does it take to cross the room?

Estimate _____   How many? _____

My estimate was

      too high   too low   reasonable

2 How many of your footprints does it take to go along the room?

Estimate _____   How many? _____

My estimate was

      too high   too low   reasonable

3 How many footprints does it take to go across your desk?

Estimate _____   How many? _____

My estimate was

       too high   too low   reasonable

4 How many footprints does it take to go all the way around the edge of your desk?

Estimate _____   How many? _____

My estimate was

       too high   too low   reasonable

5 How many footprints high is the door?

Estimate _____   How many? _____

My estimate was

       too high   too low   reasonable

Name:_____ **Date:**_____

Footprints (1b)

6 Write down some other things you can measure using your footprint and measure them.

Name of item	Estimate	How many footprints?

Name:_____ **Date:**_____

Handspans (2a)

Use your handspan to find the following:

---

1 The length of your arm

Estimate _____   How many? _____

My estimate was

      too high   too low   reasonable

---

2 The length of your leg

Estimate_____   How many? _____

My estimate was

      too high   too low   reasonable

---

3 How many handspans does it take to go across your desk?

Estimate _____   How many? _____

My estimate was

　　　　too high　　　　too low　　　　reasonable

4 How many handspans does it take to go all the way around the edge of your desk?

Estimate _____   How many? _____

My estimate was

　　　　too high　　　　too low　　　　reasonable

5 How many handspans high is the door?

Estimate _____   How many? _____

My estimate was

　　　　too high　　　　too low　　　　reasonable

Name:_____ **Date:**_____

Handspans (2b)

6 Write down some other things you can measure using
your handspan and measure them.

Name of item	Estimate	How many handspans?

Lesson M2 – Capacity

Tutor's notes

This is not a lesson to teach students the standard units of capacity (as this is taught in the Adult Numeracy core curriculum) but to help them to understand capacity. The units used are arbitrary (see Introduction to Measure p. 89).

Young children developing the concept of capacity learn through 'Free Play' with sand and water and a wide variety of objects including containers; this helps them to understand 'full', 'empty' and 'overflows'. This is then followed by 'Structured Play', at which stage containers are carefully selected to develop an understanding of 'holds less than', 'holds more than' and 'holds the same amount as'.

Some students may need experience at either or both of these stages of development, before using this lesson.

This lesson uses everyday items to help students to make sense of their adult environment. It is at this stage of development where physical units of capacity are used to link number to capacity. It draws on counting skills, the early use of a number line and estimation from the Number Tool Kit section of this book.

The capacity of a container is the measure of the amount of fluid it will hold. To develop the concept of capacity you could use water, rice or sand as your fluid.

Although students do not need to know the standard units for capacity, they should be encouraged to talk about words they have heard, or know, relating to capacity.

For the activity, you will need a variety of containers for each pair or group (see resources). Label the 250ml bottle 'A'; the 500ml bottle 'B'; the litre bottle 'C'; the 2 litre bottle 'D'; the drinks can 'E'; the drinks carton 'F'; and the cup (or mug) 'G'. Make sure that students can still clearly see the capacity on the original label, as they may want to look at this to make comparisons with their own drinks or experiences.

Diagrams can be cut out from Worksheet 1, for students to use to record their results. They may be stuck in workbooks or laminated to be used for other lessons.

During the activity, you should encourage students to use the appropriate language for capacity. Questions to ask could be 'Is this bottle full/empty?' 'Which bottle do you think holds more?' 'Which bottles hold more/less than this one?'.

Try to have some items that are not exact fractions of the larger containers to encourage the concept of 'betweenness'; see Introduction to Measure p. 89. In this case, students should be encouraged to say, 'It holds between two and three of the smaller bottles', they find this easier than saying 'It takes more than two, but less than three, small bottles to fill the big bottle'.

On Worksheet 2, students may want to write on the units of measure for each bottle. For example, they could write '250ml' on the bottle labelled 'A', '500ml' on the bottle labelled 'B', and so on.

If students have difficulty recording their answers on the worksheet, they could use bottles cut out from Worksheet 1 and stick them on to a separate piece of paper, or use laminated pictures, which you could take photographs of.

It is a good idea to take photographs of students doing the activity, to include in their records.

Criteria

Adult Pre-entry Curriculum Framework for Numeracy

Measure, shape and space: common measures

Milestone 6 – sub-element 1d
Milestone 7 – sub-element 5 and sub-element 6
Milestone 8 – sub-element 5

These elements progress to MSS1/E1.6 in the Adult Numeracy core curriculum.

P scales

Shape, space and measures   P7, P8
Using and applying mathematics   P8

Lesson M2   Capacity

Objectives

- to practice familiar language in making comparisons of capacity;
- to compare the capacity of different containers;
- to start using simple calibrated measures.

Resources

- a variety of plastic bottles and containers, for example: a milk carton, glass cleaner (with a spray top), hot water bottle, shampoo bottle and a juice bottle, drinks can, juice carton, a bucket and a kettle;

One set per group of:

- 1 × 250ml plastic bottle labelled 'A';
- 1 × 500ml plastic bottle labelled 'B';
- 1 × 1 litre plastic bottle labelled 'C';
- 1 × 2 litre plastic bottle labelled 'D';
- an empty drinks can   labelled 'E';
- an empty drinks carton   labelled 'F';
- a cup or mug   labelled 'G';
- access to water, sand or any other suitable materials to fill the bottles;
- Worksheet 1 – one per student;
- Worksheet 2 – one per student.

Lesson plan

Stage 1: Introduction and class discussion

1   Show a selection of different containers one at a time, for example, a plastic bottle, a plastic glass, a cup, a kettle, a bucket (it can be a seaside bucket), household cleaners and a hot water bottle.

Questions to ask to promote discussion:

- What do you think this is?
- What is it used for?
- How does the liquid get inside?
- How does the liquid get out again?
- How do you know when it is full?
- How do you know when it is empty?
- How will you know if it had a leak?
- What will happen if you didn't mend the leak?
- Which container will hold the most liquid when it was full?
- Which container will hold the least?

2   Have a discussion about the different liquids we see or use and the different containers we keep them in.

3   Ask students how many of the smallest containers they think it will take to fill the largest container.

4   Demonstrate, or ask students to demonstrate, to show how close their guesses were.
5   Repeat with different containers.

Activity

1   Put students into pairs or small groups and give them each a set of the labelled plastic bottles and drinks containers.
2   Encourage discussion about which ones they think will hold more/less water (or sand, or rice).
3   Explain Worksheet 2 and invite students to fill in the answers (see tutor's notes for alternative ways of recording answers). Students should be encouraged to estimate how much they think it will take to fill the bottle, before they work out the actual number.
4   Some students may be able to calibrate the bottles by marking the side with a marker pen as they complete the emptying of the smaller container into the bottle. They can then count these marks to find out how many 'smaller containerfuls' it will hold.
5   Others may be able to number the calibrations.
6   If the answer is not a whole number, they can write, or say, 'Between x and y' or 'More than x but less than y'.
7   Students should compare answers at the end of the worksheet and discuss which containers hold more than/less than each other and which hold the most and least liquid.

Worksheet 1

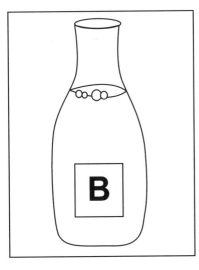

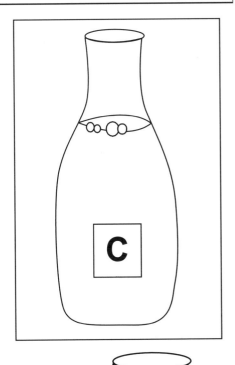

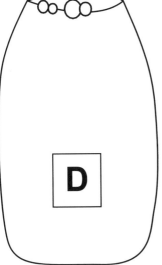

It takes ☐ of 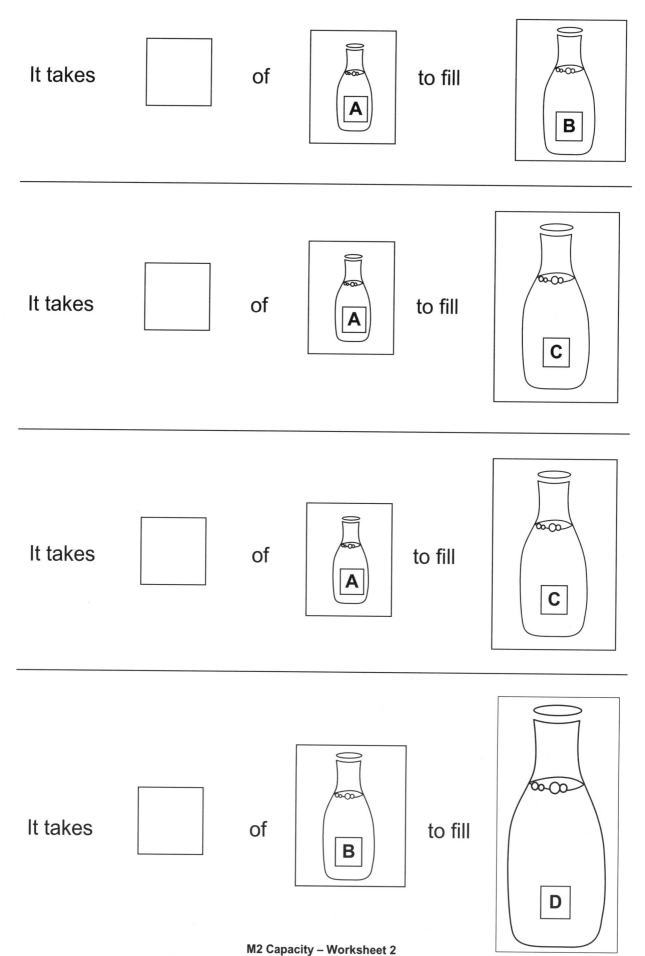 to fill

It takes ☐ of [A] to fill [B]

It takes ☐ of [A] to fill [C]

It takes ☐ of [A] to fill [C]

It takes ☐ of [B] to fill [D]

M2 Capacity – Worksheet 2
© Nadia Naggar-Smith, *Teaching Foundation Mathematics*, Routledge, 2008

It takes ☐ of 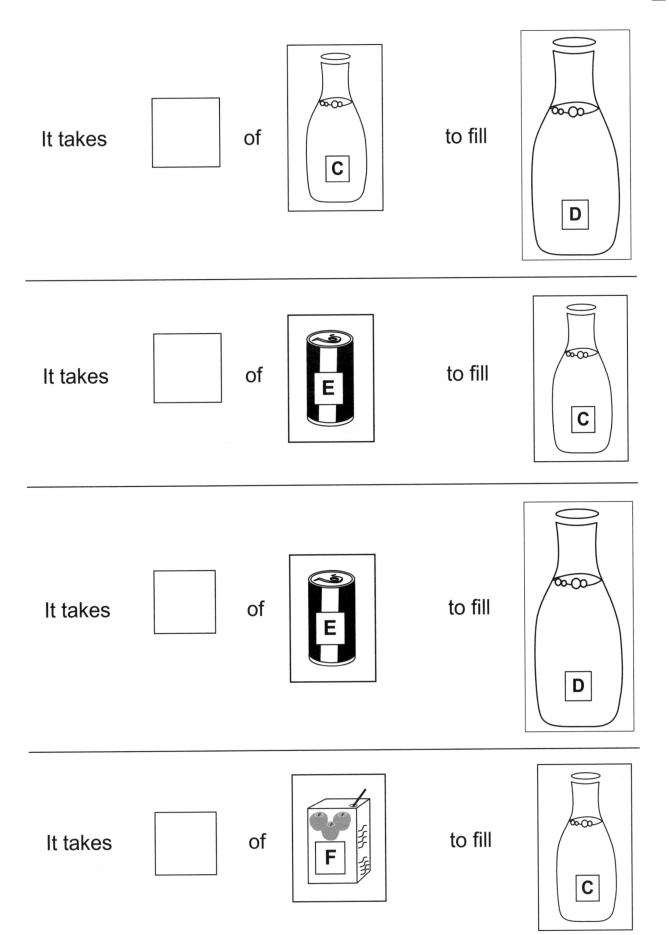 C of to fill D

It takes ☐ of E to fill C

It takes ☐ of E to fill D

It takes ☐ of F to fill C

It takes [ ] of  F of to fill 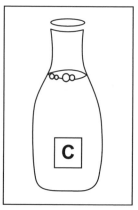 D

It takes [ ] of  G to fill  B

It takes [ ] of  G to fill 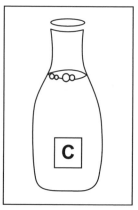 C

It takes [ ] of  G to fill  E

Lesson M3 – Shoe sizes

Tutor's notes

This activity uses British shoe sizes and the extension work on page 114 includes metric shoe sizes. The numbers used for metric shoe sizes are too large for the Adult Pre-entry Curriculum Framework, but it is useful for students to be aware of both sizes shown on their shoes. (NB: The European shoe sizes for men and women differ slightly. An average size has been used for the table on page 114.)

Part of the activity, deals with odd and even numbers; this is an important element for preparation of something they experience and should be included. One example of this is house numbers, where they are odd on one side of the road and even on the other.

For the activity, you will need to prepare a table for each student, in advance of the lesson. The table should have three columns, one for the names of all the students in the class, one for their shoe size (British) and one which is left blank (this is to be used for extension work, recording metric sizes). During the first part of the activity, the third column should be folded behind the other two, and then folded back out if needed.

You may wish to fill in the names before the lesson, or ask students to fill them in during the lesson. You should also have an OHT with the table on it, or draw one on the board for students to copy as you fill it in.

Part 2 of the activity will encourage students to practice number recall and ordering.

Students have often heard of odd and even numbers but need a memory check at the point in the lesson where they are introduced. Draw a table on the board with two columns, headed 'Odd' and 'Even'. Starting with 1 and continuing to 10 write 1 in the odd column and then 2 in the even column. Continue to do this with all of the numbers up to 10. You could also use a picture of a short street to show which side of the street are odd numbers and which side are even numbers.

If this is too abstract for your students a simple way for them to find if a number is odd or even is:

1   Place a number of items (counters) to represent the number, for example, five, on the table.
2   Position the counters in a single line.
3   Using both index fingers, at the same time, remove one counter from each end of the line.
4   Repeat this and you will find one counter remains. So five is an odd number. Even numbers do not have a remainder.

Criteria

Adult Pre-entry Curriculum Framework for Numeracy

Number

Milestone 6 – sub-element 2 and sub element 4
Milestone 7 – sub-element 2 and sub-element 3
Milestone 8 – sub-element 3 and sub-element 5

Handling data

Milestone 8 – sub-element 3 (extension work)

These elements progress to N1/E1.2 in the Adult Numeracy core curriculum.

P scales

Using and applying mathematics   P7
Number   P8

Lesson M3   Shoe sizes

Objectives

- to apply numbers to a reality situation;
- to recognise numbers;
- to introduce odd and even numbers.

If extended:

- to collect information and sort it into groups;
- to record the information collected.

Resources

- table for students to recall names and shoe sizes;
- Worksheets 1a and 1b – one per student;
- squared paper if needed for extension work;
- a number line.

Lesson plan

Stage 1: Introduction and class discussion

1   Ask students if they know what shoe size they are. Some may need to look at their shoes – they may wish to remove their shoes to look!
2   Students may have both, or either, British and metric sizes on their shoes. Encourage discussion to make students aware of the different systems.

Activity

1   Ask students to complete the table with the names of the classmates on, by writing the person's shoe size in the column next to the correct name. (This should be using British sizes, as the numbers are smaller than the metric system.) They may need to use the conversion chart on Worksheet 2. This chart may need to be extended.
2   Fill in a table on the board, or the OHT, and discuss who has the largest and smallest feet. Ask questions to promote discussion of the value of the numbers. For example, 'Does Billy have larger shoes than Jane?'; 'Which shoes are smaller, Imran's or Rosie's?' and so on.
3   Students could use their number line to look at the sizes before they give their answer.
4   Introduce the idea of odd and even numbers. (See tutor's notes.)
5   Ask if anyone has heard of odd and even numbers and encourage discussion to establish your starting point for the next part of the exercise.
6   Ask all the students who have an odd shoe size to stand and all those who have an even shoe size to sit down.
7   Once you feel students are confident with this idea, they can complete Worksheet 1.

Extension Activity 1

1   Students could create a bar chart of shoe sizes in their class.
2   Give the students pieces of paper with individual names of the class on them.
3   Using a large number line, ask students to place the names below the correct number for their shoe size.
4   This information could then be used to create a bar chart.
5   Starter questions to ask when reading the bar chart: 'Do more students take size eight shoes than size three?', 'How many students take size seven shoes?', 'How many students take size nine shoes?', 'Which is the most common size?', 'Which is the least common size?'.

Extension Activity 2

1   Introduce the second page of the worksheet.
2   Show students how to read and compare the two different sizes, and then ask them to complete the worksheet.
3   Students can now unfold the third column of the shoe size table and fill it in.

Name:_____ **Date:**_____

Shoe Sizes (1a)	

Below is a list of the shoe sizes of various students in the college.

Name	Shoe size
Susan	5
Rasheed	9
John	10
Rachel	4
Amelia	3
Mark	8
Ahmed	5
Lucy	2
Hayley	6
Ben	7

1 Which students have a shoe size that is an **odd number**?

_____   _____

_____   _____

_____

2 Which students have a shoe size that is an **even number**?

_____   _____

_____   _____

_____

Name:_____ **Date:**_____

Shoe Sizes (1b)

This chart shows the equivalent British and metric shoe sizes.

British	2	3	4	5	6	7	8	9	10
Metric	34	35	37	38	39	41	42	43	45

3 What size shoes do you wear?

British size _____

Metric size _____

4 Here is a list of the students from the previous page. Show the **metric shoe size** for each student.

Susan _____   Amelia _____

Rasheed _____   Mark _____

John _____   Ahmed _____

Rachel _____   Lucy _____

Hayley _____   Ben _____

5 Which students take an even size in metric sizes?

_____   _____

_____   _____

_____

Lesson M4 – Which coin?

Tutor's notes

The Adult Pre-Entry Curriculum Framework aims at laying firm foundations on which to build life skills and one of the basic skills in adult life is to be able to handle money when shopping (see Introduction to Number, p. 7).

Before students are introduced to value and exchange of money they need to be able to confidently recognise the coins that they are going to use. Coin recognition is a multisensory activity involving sight, touch and hearing. We identify coins in a variety of situations, for example, when we feel for them in our pockets, when we look for them in a purse, when we see them spread out before us and when we drop them on the floor.

This lesson is to familiarise students with the coins we use.

There are many resources available for money work, such as plastic coins and sticker coins, but these are only useful at the representation stage of learning when students can already identify real coins. Coin recognition requires real coins. They are identified by the way they feel, their size, shape, colour and weight. There will need to be a system in place to keep track of the coins, but remember that plastic coins can also go missing.

£2 coins are not used for this lesson, but they could be included if you wish. Once the procedures for identifying coins have been established, it is relatively easy to introduce extra coins.

A sock is used to represent a pocket in Activity 1: Feeling for money.

Criteria

Adult Pre-entry Curriculum Framework for Numeracy

Measure, shape and space: common measures

Milestone 7 – sub-element 8
Milestone 8 – sub-element 6

These elements progress to MSS1/E1.1 in the Adult Numeracy core curriculum.

P scales

Using and applying mathematics   P7

Lesson M4   Which coin?

Objectives

- to develop coin recognition through colour, shape, size and weight;
- to set firm foundations for handling money when shopping.

Resources

For each pair of students you will need:

- a selection of coins (1p, 2p, 5p, 10p, 20p, 50p, £1) and a small plastic box (a money box) to keep them in;
- a sock (for use as a pocket).

For each individual student you will need:

- a lead pencil and a brown pencil crayon;
- access to a pencil sharpener;
- a sheet of paper for making coin rubbings;
- a copy of the worksheet, 'Which Coin?'.

Lesson plan

Stage 1: Introduction and class discussion

1   Organise students into pairs and give each pair a money box.
2   Ask students which coins they know and ask them how do they know, for example, the two-pence piece is a two-pence piece and not a twenty-pence piece.
3   Discuss the differences in the coins. Look at things like what is on them (heads and tails), size, shape, colour and weight.

Activity 1

Invite your students to work in pairs and sort the coins in as many different ways as they can. You will need to lead them in this.
Examples of sorting:

- all the coins that have corners;
- all the silver coins;
- all the small coins;
- all the heavy coins;
- all the round coins.

After each sort ask if they can name the coins. Remember that they are not using values here.

Activity 2

1 Explain the object of the activity: when we feel in our pockets for money we cannot see the coins, so we have to feel for them. The sock represents your pocket.
2 Working in pairs, one person chooses a coin and puts it in the sock without the other seeing which coin it is.
3 The second person has to guess which coin it is, by touch alone, as they might do in their pocket.
4 Students should be encouraged to describe the coin's properties while they are identifying it.
5 This can be repeated as often as you feel is necessary.

Activity 3

• Still working in pairs, one person puts more than one coin into the sock and asks his/her partner to find a particular coin, for example, fifty pence.

Activity 4

1 Give out the paper and pencils and ask students to either draw around the coins or make rubbings of both sides. Use brown and silver pencils.
2 Now ask students to put a tick on all the coins that have corners and a cross on all those that do not.

Activity 5

• Ask students to complete the worksheet 'Which Coin?'.

Name:_____ **Date:**_____

Which Coin?

You will need the following coins:

1p   2p   5p   10p   20p   50p   £1

Look at the coins in front of you and answer the following questions:

1 Which coins are circles? _____

2 Which coins are a silver colour? _____

3 Which coins are copper? _____

4 Which coins have straight edges? _____

5 Which coins have corners? _____

6 Which coin is the largest, in size? _____

7 Which coin is the thickest? _____

8 Which coin feels the heaviest? _____

9 Which coin feels the lightest? _____

Lesson M5 – Weight

Tutor's notes

An inability to pick up an object is either due to its size or its weight and it is not uncommon to find students who assume these qualities are the same. Stage 1 of the lesson addresses this misconception. 'Heavy' is introduced to the students as a more discriminating term than 'bigger'.

This lesson is designed to offer opportunity for students to feel and compare weights and to demonstrate that bigger objects are not necessarily heavier.

For stage 1 of the introduction and discussion, you will need to prepare three different size boxes containing a variety of fillings, to demonstrate that weight cannot be judged solely by the size of an object. The smallest box should be the heaviest and the largest, the lightest.

Select fillings that have a distinct difference in weight, for example, a large box of polystyrene packaging and a small box containing a brick or a couple of books. If possible, all the boxes used in the first part of the introduction should be gift wrapped in the same paper. Labelling the boxes A, B and C will make discussion easier. Using boxes with mystery contents promotes discussion at the estimating and reasoning stage.

When introducing the pre-prepared boxes, be careful not to give any clues as to which box is heavier.

During stage 2 introduction and class discussion, students are making comparisons of weight between two items, thus, they are able to use their hands as balances when making a judgement about weight (this is common practice in everyday life).

The concept that 'heavier' does not always mean 'bigger' is demonstrated with a carefully chosen selection of shopping items, for example, a packet of pasta and the same size packet of rice (not the same weight), a bag of spinach and the same size bag of carrots (or similar items). The items are compared by weight. Some students may already know which of the pairs of shopping items is heavier; they may like to order three of the items from heaviest to lightest.

Labels for 'heavier' and 'lighter' should be made and placed appropriately on the items in the scale pan.

A sheet of A3 paper divided into two sets (or folded in half), one labelled 'heavier' and the other 'lighter', could be used to group the pairs of items after they have been weighed.

If you are using items that will not fit on the scale pans, you could tie some string around the item and hang them directly from the scales.

When completing Worksheet 1, students work in pairs and can use their own worksheet to record their results. Alternatively, they could put both names on one worksheet, record their findings and photocopy the completed sheets, so that they each have a record for their folder.

Criteria

Adult Pre-entry Curriculum Framework for Numeracy

Measure, shape and space: common measures

Milestone 4 – sub-element 1
Milestone 5 – sub-element 1c
Milestone 6 – sub-element 1c
Milestone 7 – sub-element 3, sub-element 4 and sub-element 6
Milestone 8 – sub-element 2 and sub-element 4

P scales

Shape, space and measures   P7, P8
Using and applying mathematics   P8

Lesson M5   Weight

Objectives

- to practice and develop the language of weight;
- to demonstrate the concept that 'bigger' does not necessarily mean 'heavier';
- to compare weights of different everyday objects.

Resources

- balancing scales, one set for each pair, or group, of students;
- a variety of objects to weigh (see tutor's notes);
- three pre-prepared different size boxes, with various fillings (see tutor's notes);
- sheet of A3 paper, divided into two sets, 'heavier' and 'lighter';
- labels: 'heavier' and 'lighter';
- copies of Worksheet 1 – one per student (see tutor's notes);
- copies of Worksheet 2 – one per student.

Lesson plan

Stage 1: Introduction and class discussion

1 Put the largest and smallest boxes of the prepared, gift-wrapped boxes, on a table at the front of the room.
2 Ask students which they think is the heavier/lighter one and discuss why.
3 Ask students to feel the boxes to see if they are correct.
4 Encourage discussion about the weight and size of the boxes.
5 Introduce the other two boxes you have prepared.
6 Ask students to tell you which they think is heaviest/lightest now.
7 Invite students to check if they are correct.
8 Discuss the findings.

Stage 2: Introduction and class discussion

1 Put two everyday items on a table at the front of the class and ask students which one they think is heavier/lighter, without touching them, and discuss why they think this.
2 Pass the items around and ask if they still think the one they thought was heavier/lighter really is.
3 Using the balance scales, weigh the items in clear view of the students and ask them which is heavier, discussing how they can check that the lower one is the heavier one.
4 Place each pair of items into the appropriate set (marked on the A3 paper) 'heavier' or 'lighter'.
5 Repeat steps 1–4, with two different items.

Activity 1

1 Give out pairs of items to each pair or group of students and ask them to say which one they think will be heavier, by looking at them, feeling the weights and then weighing them, as before.

2   During the activity, encourage students to use language such as: bigger, smaller, heavier, lighter, weighs more than, weighs less than, and so on.

3   Students will be weighing two items at a time. Ask students to put the heavier items in one set and the lighter in another (see tutor's notes).

Activity 2

1   Give out Worksheet 1 (one per student or one for each pair) and explain how to complete it.

2   Ask students to choose items around the classroom to compare and fill in the table on Worksheet 1.

Activity 3

*   Once they have completed Worksheet 1, students should be familiar with making comparisons of weights and can then be introduced to, and complete, Worksheet 2.

Name:_____ **Date:**_____

2 items I have chosen	Which is the heavier one?	Which is the lighter one?
1. 2.		
1. 2.		
1. 2.		
1. 2.		
1. 2.		

Name:_____ Date:_____

Worksheet 2
Which One is Heavier?

Draw a circle around the heavier object.

1   A person   or   A pen

2   A feather   or   A book

3   A ruler   or   A dog

4   A computer   or   A pencil

5   A bed   or   A toothbrush

6   A can of cola   or   A packet of crisps

7   A cat   or   An elephant

8   A lorry   or   A car

9   A CD   or   A television

10 A bicycle   or   A bus

© Nadia Naggar-Smith, *Teaching Foundation Mathematics*, Routledge, 2008

Lesson M6 – Time: David's Day

Tutor's notes

Order and sequence is fundamental not only to number, and many other important mathematical concepts, but also to time. Being able to read a timetable is a life skill.

At this stage in the development of concepts of time, students are ordering and sequencing daily happenings. Through use and discussion they realise that some events happen 'before' others while some happen 'after' others. The sequencing of numbers in the Number Tool Kit and their position on a number line, that is, 'before' and 'after' is applied to a pictorial time line. Daily events are also linked to hourly and half hourly times.

Students recognise 'morning', 'afternoon', 'evening' and 'night' from flashcards and practice sequencing them prior to introducing the discussion worksheet 'David's Day'. It may be necessary to start by talking about only 'daytime' and 'night' and the events that happen at these times.

The focal point of the first part of the lesson is David's Day. This helps students to join in class discussion and later, when they make their personal charts it serves as a point of reference.

Cut and paste pictures have been provided for students who are uncomfortable with drawing their own pictures.

Extension work

The concept of a circular time line – that is, 'night time' is after 'evening' and also before 'morning' – could be discussed but, as some students may find this a difficult, the work-sheet is better placed as extension work. The circular time line can be demonstrated by making a copy of David's Day into a cylinder.

The circular number line links directly to the analogue clock.

Criteria

Pre-entry Curriculum Framework for Numeracy

Measure, shape and space: common measures

Milestone 7 – sub-element 1, sub-element 2
Milestone 8 – sub-element 1b
These elements progress to MSS1/E1.2 in the Adult Numeracy core curriculum

P scales

Shape, space and measures   P8

Lesson M6   Time: David's Day

Objectives

- to recognise the names of significant times of the day;
- to relate familiar events to the significant times of the day;
- to order the events of the day on a visual daily time table.

Resources

- large Post-its and a marker;
- four large flashcards labelled morning, afternoon, evening and night;
- copies of 'David's Day' Worksheet 1 for discussion – one per student;
- copies of 'David's Day' Worksheet 2 – one per student;
- copies of Personal Day Plan (My Day) – one per student;
- cut and paste picture sheet (if needed);
- scissors;
- extension worksheets (if needed).

Lesson plan

Stage 1: Introduction and class discussion

1   Start the lesson with an inappropriate greeting – for example, 'Good night', when it is morning – and either wait for comments or invite them by stating that you have made a mistake. Ask students to tell you what you should have said.
2   Write 'morning' on a large Post-it and stick it on the board, saying 'Morning' as you do so.
3   Ask what you will say if it was afternoon and place a post-it with 'afternoon' on it on the board.
4   Repeat step 3 with 'evening' and then night, placing the Post-its in order.
5   Explain that this is the order of the day and invite students to read the words in order.
6   Show the flashcards one at a time, in random order, student reading them as they are shown.
7   Invite four students to stand in a line and hold a flashcard. Give the flashcards out in random order.
8   Now order the students so that their flashcards read in order – 'morning', 'afternoon', 'evening' and 'night'.
9   Talk about the various tasks that are done during each division of the day.

Activity 1: David's Day

1   Distribute copies of David's Day discussion sheets (Worksheet 1) amongst the students. Ideally they should work in pairs, but they may also like to have their individual worksheet to keep in their files.
2   Either point to the Post-its on the board or hold up the flashcards one at a time in order. Indicate the column headed 'morning' and ask the students what David does in the morning. Then do the same with 'afternoon', 'evening' and 'night'.
3   Now ask random questions, for example:
    'When does David phone a friend?'

'When does David get out of bed?'

'When does David watch television?'

4   Students will have heard of and may know the hours of the day in which case they may wish to link the divisions of the day to the hours of the day, for example:

'David gets up at seven o'clock in the morning'. 'Show me'.

'David goes to bed at 11 o'clock at night'. 'Show me'.

5   Distribute and explain Worksheet 2 on David's Day.

6   Students fill in Worksheet 2.

Activity 2

Distribute and explain the Personal Day Plan handout (My Day). Some students may just use pictures, some will use pictures and times, and some students may wish to colour the pictures.

Extension work

Extension work demonstrates a circular time line, that is, 'morning' comes both before 'afternoon' and after 'night'.

1   Ask students what comes before 'morning' and then demonstrate the answer by fastening a copy of the 'David's Day' worksheet to form a cylinder.

Ask further questions about the circular timeline. This links with the number lesson on number lines, before and after.

2   Distribute Worksheet 3 and assist students to fill it in.

David's Day

Morning	Afternoon	Evening	Night
7 o'clock	1 o'clock	6 o'clock	10 o'clock
Half past 7	4 o'clock	7 o'clock	11 o'clock
8 o'clock	Half past 4	8 o'clock	

M6 David's Day – Worksheet 1

Name:_____ **Date:**_____

David's Day

Look at David's day and answer the following questions

1 What time does David get up in the morning?

_____

2 What time does David eat his breakfast?

_____

3 When does David read in college?

_____

4 What time does David leave college?

_____

5 What time does David get on the bus?

_____

6 At what time does David have his tea?

_____

7 When does he watch TV?

_____

8 What time does David wash his hands
   and get ready for bed?

_____

9 When does David go to bed?

_____

10 What time do you get up?

_____

My Day

Morning	Afternoon	Evening	Night

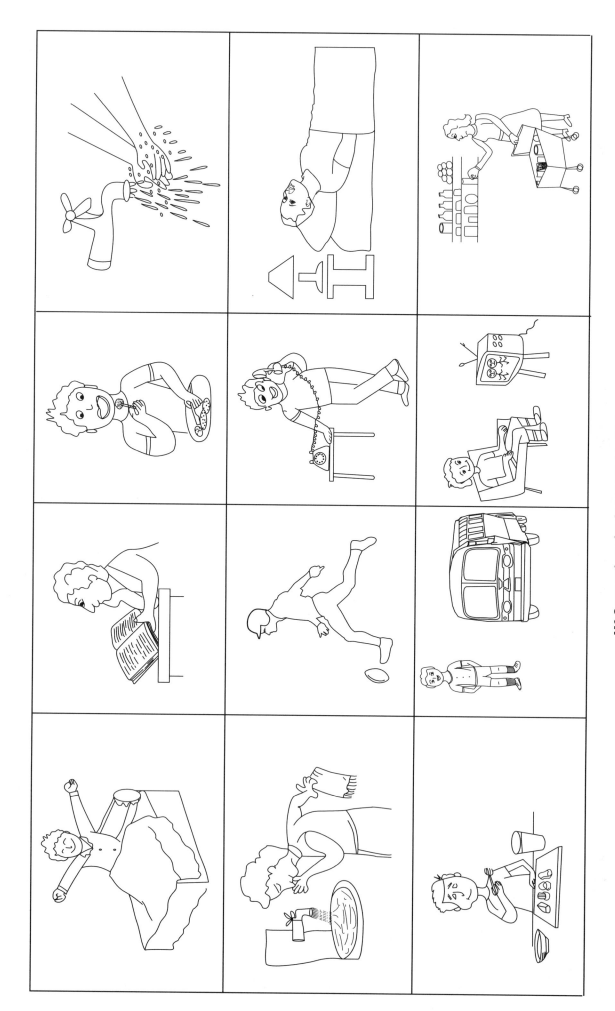

Name:_____ **Date:**_____

Circular Timeline

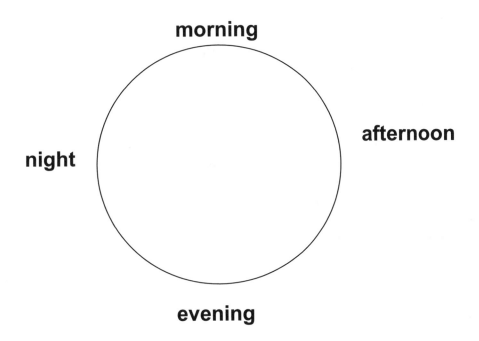

morning

afternoon

night

evening

1 _____ comes **before** evening

2 _____ comes **before** morning

3 _____ comes **before** night

4 _____ comes **after** evening

5 _____ comes **after** night

6 _____ comes **after** afternoon

Lesson M7 – Days of the week

Tutor's notes

Many students will already know some of the days of the week. They will know their names when they hear them, when they see them written down, or both. Consistently sequencing them correctly is more challenging, as it requires sequencing ability and ability to commit them to memory.

This lesson offers a multisensory approach to strengthening these abilities.

The flashcards should be made from different coloured cards, with the letters written in bold black for strong contrast. Colour is a good visual aid to memory. You will see students closing their eyes when they are trying to remember the days of the week; they are trying to visualise the flashcards.

Stage 1 of the lesson helps students to remember the days of the week by stimulating visual and auditory senses. It personalises them and identifies the small word 'day' in them, to help with reading and spelling.

Activity 1 uses the tactile skill of writing, to strengthen the learning in stage 1 of the lesson.

Activity 2 applies previous experience from the Number Tool Kit of 'before' and 'after' (number lines) to days of the week.

Criteria

Adult Pre-entry Curriculum for Numeracy

Measure, shape and space: common measures

Milestone 7 – sub-element 1 and sub-element 2
Milestone 8 – sub-element 1

P scales

Using and applying mathematics   P8
Number   P8
Space, shape and measures   P8

Lesson M7   Days of the week

Objectives

- to read days of the week;
- to write days of the week;
- to order days of the week;
- to memorise days of the week;
- to apply knowledge of 'before' and 'after' from the Number Tool Kit to days of the week;
- to apply knowledge of cardinal numbers from the Number Tool Kit to days of the week;
- to use a simple time table.

Resources

- seven large flashcards, one for each day of the week (using different coloured cards for each day, or different coloured writing for each day, is a good memory aid);
- Worksheets 1a and 1b – one per student;
- Worksheet 2 – one per student;
- Worksheet 3a and 3b – one per student.

Lesson plan

Stage 1: Introduction and class discussion

1   Ask your students what day it is and then hold up the appropriate flashcard:
- Ask students what the first letter is and draw their attention to the fact that it is the name of the day and all names start with a capital letter.
- Talk about their own names and how they start with a capital letter.
- Remind them that all 'special names' begin with a capital letter.

2   Look at the flashcard again and ask, 'Who can find the "day" in it?'
3   Now hold up the other days of the week (in any order) and encourage students to read the name of the day. Emphasise the 'day' part, as they say it.
4   Next, assist students to sequence the flashcards into days of the week.

Activity 1

1   Hand out Worksheet 1a, 'Days of the Week', and remind students of the 'day' part of the days.
2   Invite students to fill in Worksheet 1a.
3   Once they have completed 1a, they can then complete Worksheet 1b.

Activity 2

1   Hand out Worksheet 2, 'After and Before'.
2   Explain how to complete the worksheet and ask the students to work in pairs to fill it in.

Activity 3

1   Ask students how they know which lessons they have each day of the week and talk about the usefulness of a timetable.
2   Give each student a copy of Nagwa's timetable (Worksheet 3a).
3   Discuss the abbreviations used for the days of the week, reminding students of Worksheet 1 and drawing their attention to the way days are abbreviated.
4   On Nagwa's timetable, the days Monday to Friday are abbreviated. Ask students how Saturday and Sunday will be abbreviated.
5   Discuss the various lessons Nagwa has and the days of the week she has them on. Show them how to work out on which day she has the lessons.
6   Show students how to complete Worksheet 3b and ask them to answer the questions. Students may work alone, or in pairs for this activity.

Extension work

Bring in a selection of articles with abbreviated dates on them for students to search for the day abbreviations.

| Sunday |
| Monday |
| Tuesday |
| Wednesday |
| Thursday |
| Friday |
| Saturday |

Name:_____ **Date:**_____

Below are the days of the week. Fill in the missing parts of the names.

Sun_____
Mon_____
Tues_____
Wed___ s_____
Thurs_____
Fri_____
Sat__ r_____

Wednesday

Sunday

Thursday

Tuesday

Saturday

Monday

Friday

Name:_____ **Date:**_____

Worksheet 1b
Days of the Week

Use **Worksheet 1a** to answer the following questions

1 How many days of the week start with the letter S? _____

2 How many days of the week start with the letter M?_____

3 How many days of the week start with the letter T? _____

4 How many days of the week start with the letter W?_____

5 How many days are there in one week? _____

6 Today is _____

7 Tomorrow will be _____

8 Yesterday was _____

9 Which two days we do call **'the weekend'**?

_____ and _____

Name:_____ **Date:**_____

Worksheet 2
Days of the Week

After

1 Which day comes **after** Monday? _____

2 Which day comes **after** Wednesday? _____

3 Which day comes **after** Tuesday? _____

4 Which day comes **after** Friday? _____

5 Which day comes **after** Thursday? _____

Before

1 Which day comes **before** Friday? _____

2 Which day comes **before** Saturday? _____

3 Which day comes **before** Tuesday? _____

4 Which day comes **before** Monday? _____

5 Which day comes **before** Wednesday? _____

Nagwa's Timetable

	Mon.	Tues.	Wed.	Thurs.	Fri.
9:00 – 10:30	Communications	Maths	I.C.T.	Art	
Break					
11:00 – 12:30	Maths		Communications		Life skills
Break					
1:30 – 3:00		French	Music		Sport
Break					
3:30 – 5:00	I.C.T.	Life skills		Science	

Study Period – No Lesson

M7 Days of the Week – Worksheet 3a (Nagwa's Timetable)
© Nadia Naggar-Smith, *Teaching Foundation Mathematics*, Routledge, 2008

Name:_____ **Date:**_____

Worksheet 3b
Nagwa's Timetable

Look at Nagwa's timetable and answer the following questions.

1 On which day does Nagwa have a French lesson?

_____

2 On which day does Nagwa have an Art lesson?

_____

3 On which days does Nagwa have I.C.T. lessons?

_____ and _____

4 On which days does Nagwa have Maths lessons?

_____ and _____

5 On which days does Nagwa have Communications lessons?

_____ and _____

6 On which days does Nagwa have a Sports lesson?

_____

7 On which day does Nagwa have a Music lesson?

_____

Lesson M8 – Months of the year

Tutor's notes

This lesson is a sequel to the lesson on days of the week and demonstrates how the days fit into the months. It helps students to understand calendars and diaries in life skills.

The lessons are progressive, like most of the lessons in this book, and students should work at their own pace and to only one step beyond their comfort zone.

Part 1 of the lesson uses a calendar to assess, through guided discussion, the knowledge and understanding of months of the year that students have already mastered. It forms links between days of the week and months of the year.

Activity 1 prepares students for the recording involved in Worksheet 1b, 'Days of the Month'.

Worksheet 2 is a problem-solving worksheet; the previous activities are now presented in context and require students to read, think and do. If students work in pairs for this activity, they can help each other with the reading and writing involved.

The final part of Worksheet 1b uses cardinal numbers from the Number Tool Kit and applies them to life skills. Students may need reminding of the cardinal numbers but first leave them to see if they can make the links for themselves – this strengthens their long term memory.

Activity 2 prepares students for word problems related to Worksheet 2, 'About Fred'.

You may need to highlight the questions, to make access easier for students who need to revisit the question frequently. Some students do this because they are under-confident in their reading ability; others because they find difficulty holding the question in their head whilst looking back at the calendar. All students should refer to the question to check that they have done what they were asked to do.

All of the skills introduced in this lesson prepare students for moving forward into Basic Skills problem-solving activities.

Activity 3 uses cardinal numbers from the Number Tool Kit and applies these numbers to months of the year. It prepares students for finding the month of the year in dates presented in number format, for example, 12/10/2008.

Criteria

Adult Pre-entry Curriculum Framework for Numeracy

Measure, shape and space: common measures

Milestone 7 – sub-element 1

These elements progress to MSS1/E1.2 in the Adult Numeracy core curriculum.

P scales

Number	P8
Shape, space and measures	P8

Lesson M8   Months of the year

Objectives

- to connect days of the week to months of the year;
- to use cardinal numbers in reality situations;
- to understand problem solving;
- to reinforce the understanding of diaries;
- to understand timing of events.

Resources

- one large calendar (any year);
- Worksheet 1a, 'January' – one per student;
- Worksheet 1b, 'Reading a Calendar' – one per student;
- Worksheet 2, 'About Fred' – one per student;
- Worksheet 3, 'Months of the Year' – one per student.

Lesson plan

Stage 1: Introduction and class discussion

1   Show your students a large calendar and ask if anyone knows what it is. Be guided by their response and ask questions such as: 'Do you have a calendar?', 'What do you use it for?', 'Where do you keep it?', 'What else can you tell me about it?'. Some students will have a diary with a calendar in; it helps them to use it, where practical, throughout the activities.
2   Ask one student when his or her birthday is and find that month in the calendar.
3   Explain how the days are set out in that month.
4   Invite the birthday student either to find their birthday month on the calendar, or to nominate a friend to find it for them.
5   Repeat steps 2–4 with different students.

Activity 1

1   Hand out a copy of Worksheet 1a, 'Days of the Month', to each student.
2   Explain that they have a page out of a calendar, and that it is for the month of January. Ask the students to read, out loud, the days of the week.
3   Show students how to find the number of, for example, Wednesdays in the month. You will need to demonstrate several further examples, before students can fill in the first part of the worksheet.
4   Hand out a copy of Worksheet 1b, 'Days of the Month', to each student.
5   Show them which part of the worksheet they are going to fill in (the number of days in the month) and assist them to complete the statements.
6   The second part of the worksheet uses and applies ordinal numbers to the days of the month. Students who feel that they can answer these questions may do so.

Activity 2

1   Ask your students if they play sports or attend a club each week. Talk about the days and number of days they attend each week.
2   Ask volunteers to come and count how many days they attend their club each month, starting with those who only attend once a week.
3   Now students complete the statements on Worksheet 1a.
4   Students may also fill in the second part of the worksheet, if they wish to do so.

Activity 3

Introduce Worksheet 2, 'About Fred', and assist students to complete it.

Activity 4

1   Hand out Worksheet 3, one to each student. This worksheet uses word problems and students should work in pairs, to help each other to read them.
2   Explain the worksheet to your students and assist them to fill them in, where and when necessary.

January					
Sunday		7	14	21	28
Monday	1	8	15	22	29
Tuesday	2	9	16	23	30
Wednesday	3	10	17	24	31
Thursday	4	11	18	25	
Friday	5	12	19	26	
Saturday	6	13	20	27	

M8 Months of the Year – Worksheet 1a
© Nadia Naggar-Smith, *Teaching Foundation Mathematics*, Routledge, 2008

Name:_____ **Date:**_____

Worksheet 1b
Reading a Calendar

Look at the calendar for January and complete the following:

1 There are _____ Wednesdays in January.

2 There are _____ Saturdays in January.

3 There are _____ Sundays in January.

4 There are _____ Fridays in January.

5 There are _____ Tuesdays in January.

6 There are _____ Mondays in January.

7 There are _____ Thursdays in January.

8 What **day** is 1st January? _____

9 What **day** is 5th January? _____

10 What **day** is 10th January? _____

11 What **day** is 7th January? _____

12 What **day** is the last day of January? _____

Name: _____ **Date:** _____

Worksheet 2
About Fred

This is Fred.

Using your calendar for January, answer the questions below.

1 Fred's birthday is on 4th January. What **day** is his birthday on?

   _____

2 He has fish and chips only on Fridays. How many times does he have fish and chips in January?

   _____

3 He has a ballet class every Wednesday. How many times does he have ballet classes in January?

   _____

4 He goes to computer club every Monday. How many times does he go to computer club in January?

   _____

Name:_____ **Date:**_____

Worksheet 3
Months of the Year

Here are the months of the year:

1 January	**7 July**
2 February	**8 August**
3 March	**9 September**
4 April	**10 October**
5 May	**11 November**
6 June	**12 December**

1 There are_____ months in a year.

2 The 1st month is _____.

3 The last month is _____.

4 The 2nd month is _____.

5 The 5th month is _____.

6 The 3rd month is _____.

7 The 4th month is _____.

8 The month after July is _____.

9 The month before October is _____.

10 My birthday is in _____.

11 This is the _____ month.

Lesson M9 – Strings and things (using the language of length)

Tutor's notes

This lively, problem-solving activity involves exactly matching measuring strings to objects.

The first part of the lesson provides students with a clear explanation of what is to be done during the activity. Discussion between student and teacher encourages students to rehearse the language of length, clear any misunderstandings and build confidence.

During the activity, students have opportunities to discuss the activity themselves and make decisions. They are given worksheets, on which to record their results. This encourages them to re-examine their results and to see that they present the best possible answer.

When the group re-forms, students are encouraged to use their results in remembering what they did. Verbalisation helps students to organise their thinking and is a valuable problem-solving technique for Basic Skills.

The early problem-solving techniques being developed during this lesson are:

- identifying the task;
- discussing the task;
- starting the task;
- doing the task;
- recording;
- discussing the recording.

This order of problem solving will be further developed in Basic Skills.

The extension work strengthens both concepts of length and problem-solving techniques.

Criteria

Adult Pre-entry Curriculum Framework for Numeracy

Measure, shape and space: common measures

Milestone 5 – sub-element 1
Milestone 6 – sub-element 1
Milestone 8 – sub-element 3

P scales

Shape, space and measures   P7, P8
Using and applying mathematics   P7

Lesson M9   Strings and things (using the language of length)

Objectives

- to practice problem solving;
- to practice practical measuring;
- to compare length;
- to discuss;
- to record results.

Resources

- five lengths of string;
- masking tape;
- coloured pens;
- Worksheet 1 – strings and things – one per student.

Lesson Plan

Before you start the lesson, you will need to mark five objects along one edge with the masking tape, to show the students which objects they will be using for this activity. For example, place a piece of masking tape along the vertical edge of a cupboard.

Each length of masking tape on the object to be used should have a number on it: 1, 2, 3, 4 or 5.

Cut five lengths of string to match the length of the masking tape on each object exactly. On each string make a masking tape tag, each with a different coloured spot on it. You can make these by folding a piece of tape over the string. Alternatively, you could use letters instead of colours on the tags.

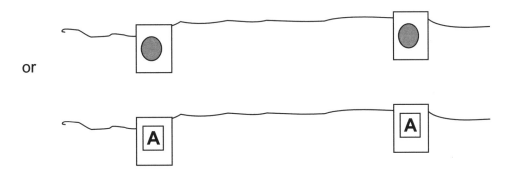

Ideally, you will need a set of five tapes for each pair of students.

Stage 1: Introduction and class discussion

1   Explain that the group is going to solve some problems today. Show them the masking tape marking the edges of the five objects in the room and read the numbers on each one. Make sure that students can name the objects.

2   Now show them the strings and explain how one string, and only one, matches the length of the tape on your chosen object. They are going to have to solve the problem of which string matches which tape.

3   Promote discussion by showing the tape on one of the objects and then holding up different strings and asking, 'Is this the right one?' each time. Invite students to come out and test it, encouraging them to say, 'too long', 'too short' or 'exactly right'.

Activity 1

1   Students find a partner.
2   Give each pair of students a set of strings and ask them to match the strings to the objects. There is no recording at this stage.

Activity 2

1   Hand out Worksheet 1. Each student should have his or her own recording sheet.
2   Explain how to complete the worksheet. You may need to set a time limit within which to work.
3   Students should now record which string matches each object.

Activity 3

Draw the whole group together and encourage individuals to tell the rest of the group what they did and discuss their results.

Extension work

Repeat this activity, changing the items used.

Name:_____ **Date:**_____

Strings and Things

Record your answers here.

Number on tape	Colour of spots
1	◯
2	◯
3	◯
4	◯
5	◯

Name:_____ **Date:**_____

<table>
<tr><td colspan="2" align="center">Strings and Things</td></tr>
</table>

Record your answers here.

Number on tape	Letter on string
1	
2	
3	
4	
5	

Lesson M10 – Addition and subtraction, using money

Tutor's notes

At this learning level, adult learners have often spent many years seeing and using symbols that lack meaning. The Adult Pre-entry Curriculum Framework structures the curriculum to follow for these students and, for mainstream schools, best fit level descriptors for assessment of achievement are set by P scales; both guide learners to understand the concepts of mathematics, without worrying about the symbols.

The connecting of symbols to concepts (the connecting level) offers opportunity for learners to see the symbols that visually represent the concepts they have explored. This connecting of symbols is a crucial step in the development of a 'tool kit' to use in the basic skills of every-day life. If the concepts have been well formed, it should not be a lengthy process.

This lesson is presented at the 'connecting' level and moves gradually through to recording:

1 language only;
2 recording using tick boxes;
3 recording using symbols;
4 extension work involving three symbols: =, −, +.

Money problems should be closely linked to progress in number and ideally linked to shopping situations but, at this stage, students are only working with low numbers and it is difficult to find reality situations. Playing and recording games is a good way of developing this concept. Traditional activities with adding and subtracting 1p can just as easily be done with £1 coins and seem to be more acceptable to mature students.

The board game used in this lesson uses £1 coins, but can just as easily be used with 1p coins. The worksheets can be used with either of the coins.

Students usually find it easier to read the £ sign than to write it. When using the worksheets, you could fill in the £ sign for them or you could help them to write their own. If you use the symbol on your computer keyboard it is easily described and written as a letter 'f' with a foot on it.

The worksheets are progressive and only introduced after the students are fluent with playing the game.

Worksheet 1 is a simple tick box introducing appropriate recording of the use of + and −. This simple recording should not interrupt the playing of the game.

Worksheet 2 requires students to appropriately record + and − (subtraction at this stage only involves taking away). Students record how many they added or took away (in this case it will always be 1).

Worksheet 3 requires students to use = , −, + signs.

* The first column is for the number of turns.
* The second column shows how much the student has before each toss of the die. The fact that this is always the same number as the last column on the line above provokes discussion of a simple number pattern.

Students will always be able to count the coins, watching them increase and decrease. Where necessary, students may use calculators.

Students should only work as far as their interest and ability are comfortably accommodated. The lesson will need to be introduced over several lessons and revisited.

The game

To set up the game

- You will need a copy of the 'track' to be found at the end of the lesson. This can be enlarged and laminated to reuse.
- Ten coins to place on the squares with the dots on.
- Three coins for each player.
- One counter or plastic bottle top for each player.

To play the game

1   Taking it in turns, students throw the die and move their counter the required number of places along the track.
2   If there is a coin in the box they land on, the student collects it. If the player lands on a box where there is no coin, he or she must place one of their coins there.
3   The student then records this on their worksheet by adding or subtracting £1 from the amount they started with, on that turn.

To finish the game

The game finishes when all of the players have crossed the finishing line.

To win the game

The player with the largest amount of money is the winner.

Criteria

Adult Pre-entry Curriculum Framework for Numeracy

Measure, shape and space: common measures

Milestone 6 – sub-element 3
Milestone 7 – sub-element 6 and sub-element 8
Milestone 8 – sub-element 5, sub-element 7 and sub-element 10

P scales

Using and applying mathematics   P8
Number   P8

Lesson M10   Addition and subtraction, using money

Objectives

- to use understanding of numbers to play games;
- to record results;
- to connect concepts to symbols;
- to use addition and subtraction signs;
- to use the equals sign.

Resources

- the game board, or track (one for each pair of students);
- one regular die, with 1–6 on it;
- ten coins to place on the game board;
- three coins for each player;
- a counter, button or plastic bottle top for each player;
- Worksheet 1 – one per student;
- Worksheet 2 – one per student;
- extension worksheets (if needed).

Lesson plan

Stage 1: Introduction and class discussion

1   Show students a £1 coin and ask if they know how much it is worth.
2   Discuss what you could buy with the coin, to give an idea of value.
3   Ask if anyone knows how to write £1. If they do, ask them to write it either on the board, or on paper, and show it to the group.
4   Show students how to write the £ sign (see tutor's notes).
5   Introduce the money game and show students how to play the game (see tutor's notes).

Activity 1

1   Students should initially work in pairs. This makes their turn come around more frequently and promotes discussion.
2   Place the ten coins on the board.
3   Give each student three coins.
4   Select the person who is going to start and begin the game.
5   Play the game.
6   Repeat steps 1 to 5 until the students are fluent with the game.
7   You may wish to increase the number of players at this stage (no more than four).

Activity 2

1   Introduce Worksheet 1 and show students how to use it.
2   Students play the game and fill the worksheet. They may need to practice with a single game sheet (one per game) until they are confident enough to have their own individual sheet.

Activity 3

1   Introduce Worksheet 2 and explain how to use it.
2   Students now play the game and fill in the worksheet.

Activity 4

1   Introduce Worksheet 3 and explain how to use it.
2   Students now play the game and fill in the worksheet.

Extension work

Using both £1 and £2 coins (or 1p and 2p coins) provides a more challenging game.

START

FINISH

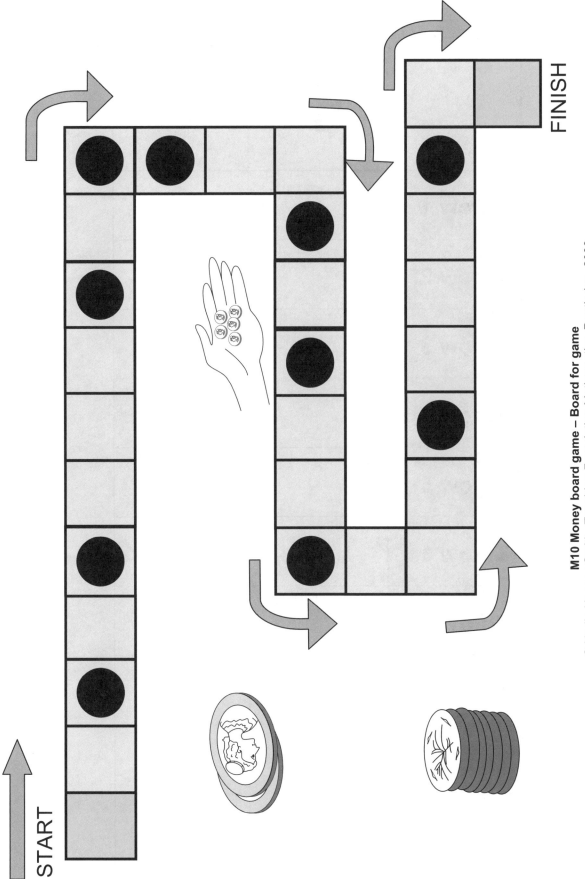

M10 Money board game – Board for game
© Nadia Naggar-Smith, *Teaching Foundation Mathematics*, Routledge, 2008

Name:_____ **Date:**_____

Tick the box

	+	**−**
Throw 1		
Throw 2		
Throw 3		
Throw 4		
Throw 5		
Throw 6		
Throw 7		
Throw 8		
Throw 9		
Throw 10		

Name:_____ **Date:**_____

	+ or –	**How many?**
Throw 1		
Throw 2		
Throw 3		
Throw 4		
Throw 5		
Throw 6		
Throw 7		
Throw 8		
Throw 9		
Throw 10		

Name:_____ **Date:**_____

	How many £s?				

	I am starting with	+ or –		=	At the end I have
Throw 1					
Throw 2					
Throw 3					
Throw 4					
Throw 5					
Throw 6					
Throw 7					
Throw 8					
Throw 9					
Throw 10					

Part III
Shape

Introduction to Shape

The language of shape

Ideally, students should move through four stages of developing abstract thinking when learning about shapes, which are:

1   physical experience;
2   language to describe that experience;
3   representation;
4   symbolisation.

Too often the first language to which they have been introduced is names such as 'triangle', 'square', 'rectangle' and 'circle'. These words are purely symbolic labels, symbolising a set of concepts of that shape. The word 'triangle' should bring to mind a visual image of different types and orientation of triangles. If the concepts have not been developed through stages 1, 2 and 3, the shape names are unlikely to be used and applied in everyday life.

   Although it is important to use the correct terminology in mathematics, students may have developed their own simplified language to describe shapes. Therefore, they should initially be allowed to use their own language, as this encourages student participation in the lesson. It is then helpful to link students' language to the correct terminology. For example, when you introduce a triangle you could say 'This shape, which is like a "Dairylea" cheese, is called a . . . ' and let students supply the word 'triangle'.

   At this level of concept development, students learn to discriminate between shapes by comparing one shape with another. Faces are found to be flat or curved; edges to be straight or curved; the different number of faces, edges and corners are counted and compared. Differences are investigated and similarities are established. The lessons in this section of the book have been developed to provide opportunities for students to match familiar words to shapes. The words most commonly used are 'flat', 'round', 'curved', 'corner', 'edge', 'surface' and 'face'.

   Students learn to describe shapes by:

*   naming;
*   looking for similarities;
*   looking for differences.

   Students are encouraged to:

*   discuss;
*   visualise;
*   relate shapes to everyday situations.

3D shape

Students will have had previous experience of feeling and observing solid shapes and may remember some of the shape names. Whether to start teaching shape with 3D or 2D shapes is a debatable point, but it is often easier to link reality situations to three-dimensional objects, they are easier for students to handle and provide opportunity to learn through a multisensory approach. Technically, you cannot pick up a 2D shape, but tutors often use thin plastic plane shapes to demonstrate 2D. Although the lessons in this section of the book start with 3D shape, the teaching order can be changed to meet the preference of individual tutors.

Multisensory learning

We all use our five senses in different ways to help us to remember and recall facts and there are three main learning styles involving the senses.

1   Visual learners, who like to see things written down, look at pictures and objects and watch demonstrations. Shape and colour are also important to these learners.
2   Auditory learners, who like explanations, repeating names and words.
3   Tactile learners, who like to touch things and move them around.

Students have different strengths and weaknesses in their ability to use their senses to help them to learn. It is therefore important to offer a variety of multisensory learning experiences.

Many (but not all) students find working with shapes less of a challenge than number work. For these students, the motivation that grows from success and enjoyment of the topic has a positive effect on learning in other areas of mathematics.

Lesson S1 – Make a shape

Tutor's notes

You may wish to spread these activities out over several lessons, or even over a period of time. Activity sequence 1 to 5 is repeated with each new shape and the order of introduction is:

- sphere;
- cube;
- cuboid;
- cylinder.

The cone is the final shape and no guidance is given with this as it is a 'problem solving' activity. Simply ask your students to make a cone.

At pre-entry level students do not need to know the correct names for the three-dimensional shapes (they may use 'ball' for spheres and 'box' for cubes and cuboids. These names are a good starting point, but students will need to learn the correct names at entry level 1 (MSS2/E1.1)). It is useful for the students to be familiar with the correct names from an early stage in their learning. If they are not, they will have to learn new words for shapes, at a later stage and this could become confusing for them.

Criteria

Adult Pre-entry Curriculum Framework for Numeracy

Measure, shape and space: shape and space

Milestone 7 – sub-element 2
Milestone 8 – sub-element 2 and sub-element 3

Both these elements progress to MSS2/E1.1 in the Adult Numeracy core curriculum.

P scales

Using and applying mathematics   P7
Shape, space and measures   P7, P8

Lesson S1   Make a shape

Objectives

- to describe properties of shapes;
- to learn names of shapes.

Resources

- a ball of plasticine for each student;
- one of each of the following solid shapes: sphere, cube, cuboid, cylinder and cone.

Lesson plan

Stage 1: Introduction and class discussion

1   Give each student a ball of plasticine and ask him or her to roll it in their hands to make it soft.
2   Put the **sphere** where it is in clear view of each student.
3   Tell the students the name of the shape and ask them what they can tell you about it. Encourage them to feel the shape, smell it and talk about its colour.
4   Now ask them to make the shape (a sphere) out of their plasticine and whisper its name, whilst they are making it. (This is a multisensory way to help them to remember shape names.)
5   Take votes on who has made the best shape.

Activity

1   Put the **sphere** back in the box. Lift the **cube** out of the box and place it in a position where it is in clear view of each student.
2   Tell the students the name of the shape and ask them to repeat it.
3   Ask them to look at their sphere and tell you if it is the 'same' or 'different' to the cube and why.
4   Now ask them to make their plasticine sphere into a cube and whisper its name, whilst they are doing so.
5   Discuss what they had to do to make the sphere into a cube.
6   Ask them to show you the corners.
7   Ask them to show you the edges.
8   Ask them how many corners a cube has.
9   Ask them how many edges a cube has.

Lesson S2 – The feely box

Tutor's notes

As the objectives for this activity are matching and observing, it is not necessary to use shape names at this stage but it may be helpful if names are mentioned.

Criteria

Adult Pre-entry Curriculum Framework for Numeracy

Measure, shape and space: shape and space

Milestone 7 – sub-element 2
Milestone 8 – sub-elements 2, 3 and 4

Both these elements progress to MSS1/E1.3 and MSS1/E1.4 in the Adult Numeracy core curriculum.

P scales

Using and applying mathematics   P7
Shape, space and measures   P7, P8

Lesson S2   The feely box

Matching shapes

Objectives

- to match shapes observing similarities and differences;
- to link everyday objects to solid shapes.

Resources

Two each of the following:

- **everyday items**: small and medium boxes, tins, and packets, for example: plastic storage boxes, match boxes, Smartie tubes, toilet roll middles, cereal packages, tins.
- **solid shapes**: spheres, cubes, cylinders, cuboids.

One of the following:

- **'Feely Box'**: a large box and a hand towel.

Lesson plan

Stage 1: Introduction and class discussion

1   Place four or five pairs of objects on a table at the front of the room.
2   Allow the students time to examine the objects and ask questions.

Activity

1   Divide the objects into two identical sets. Explain what you are doing.
2   Place one set of objects in the large box (the 'Feely Box'). Cover it with a towel and place the box at one end of the table (explain).
3   Spread the remaining objects over the table.
4   Ask for a volunteer to select a shape from the table and examine it. Then ask the volunteer to feel inside the 'Feely Box' and find the partner for his or her shape.
5   The two shapes are placed side by side and students are asked: 'Was the volunteer right or wrong?' 'How do you know?'
6   You could vary this by putting the solid shapes in the box and asking a volunteer to select an everyday item.
7   A second student should then select the solid shape from the 'Feely Box', which matches the object (or vice versa).
8   Once they have matched the solid shape and everyday items, the students should then discuss which one is longer, shorter, bigger, smaller, and so on.

Options

You may wish to continue this activity for the remainder of the lesson or your students may benefit from working in pairs or small groups to continue the activity.

Lesson S3 – Catch the shape

Tutor's notes

This lesson has been designed to provide students with the opportunity to use rapid recognition of shapes and to name those shapes.

The purpose of the shape name cards (during stage 1 of the lesson) is to provide an opportunity for the pupils to read the names of the shapes and/or to look at the word patterns formed by the shape names.

It is sometimes helpful to look at how the names are formed, for example, cube and cuboid. Students can listen for the word 'cube' in 'cuboid' and then match the first three letters. Discussing the fact that 'cuboid' is a longer or 'more stretched out' word than 'cube'. Comparing the shapes with their written names will help students to remember which shape name belongs to which shape.

Criteria

Adult Pre-entry Curriculum Framework for Numeracy

Measure, shape and space: shape and space

Milestone 7 – sub-element 2

This element progresses to MSS2/E1.1 in the Adult Numeracy core curriculum.

P scales

Using and applying mathematics   P6, P7
Shape, space and measures   P8

Lesson S3   Catch the shape

Objective

* to name shapes (sphere, cube, cuboid).

Resources

* a sphere (tennis ball);
* a cube (fluffy dice);
* a cuboid (foam);
* three shape name cards (sphere, cube, cuboid).

Lesson plan

Stage 1: Introduction and class discussion

1   Pass the shapes around the class and let each student examine them.
2   Place the shapes on a table and say the name of each one as you place its written name in front of it. At this stage students are using a multisensory approach to memorising shape names:

* tactile: feeling the shapes.
* auditory: listening to the sound of the shape name.
* visual: looking at the shapes and reading the shape names.

3   Encourage students to say the shape names (using oral motor skills) and listen to their own voices saying the name.

Activity

1   Invite students to form a circle.
2   Give the sphere, the cube and the cuboid to three different students.
3   The students are now going to throw the shapes around the circle and the person who catches a shape holds it up and calls out the name of that shape.

This needs organisation, here is a suggestion:

1   Tutor shouts out the name of a shape, for example, 'sphere'.
2   The student holding the sphere then shouts out the name of the person to whom he or she will like to throw the shape and the name of the shape. e.g. 'Molly: sphere'.
3   The named student (Molly) then catches the shape, holds it up and says its name (sphere).
4   Repeat stages 1 to 3 as often as needed.
5   At the end of this activity discuss which was the easiest shape to catch and why. If the shapes are dropped, discuss which ones rolled or slid.

If students have poor motor skills, the tutor should pass the shape to the person whom the student selects.

Lesson S4 – Roll the shapes

Tutor's notes

The previous lessons in this book on shape have all been designed to provide physical experience of shapes and to develop language to describe those experiences. This lesson moves students on towards recording.

Worksheets can be placed in the student's file and used for record purposes.

Criteria

Adult Pre-entry Curriculum Framework for Numeracy

Measure, shape and space: shape and space

Milestone 7 – sub-element 4
Milestone 8 – sub-element 2 and 5

P scales

Using and applying mathematics   P6, P7
Shape, space and measures   P8

Lesson S4   Roll the shapes

Objective

- to develop an ability to sort and classify 3D shapes and describe their properties.

Resources

- a box of solid shapes (sphere, cube, cuboid, cylinder, cone);
- a sloping surface (for rolling shapes down);
- Worksheet: '*What will this shape do?*' (one for each student).

Lesson plan

Stage1: Introduction and class discussion

1 Place the shapes in full view of the students.
2 Questions to ask: 'Which of these shapes is best for rolling?', 'Why?', 'Which is best for building?', 'Why?', 'What could you build with this shape?'
3 Demonstrate how to make the slope for rolling (you could use a pile of books and a board) and introduce the activity sheet.

Activity

To promote discussion and use of mathematical language, students should work in pairs or small groups.

1 Students build a slope and select their shapes.
2 Using the '*What will this shape do?*' worksheet students should experiment with rolling, sliding and building.
3 The students should record their results on the worksheet by placing a cross or a tick in the appropriate box.

Name: _____   Date: _____

What will this shape do?

Shape	Will it roll?	Will it slide?	Will it spin?	Can you build with it?
Sphere				
Cube				
Cuboid				
Cylinder				
Cone				

S4 Roll the Shapes – Worksheet (What will this shape do?)

Lesson S5 – 3D shapes in our lives

Tutor's notes

This activity encourages students to use visual memory. It may be helpful if they close their eyes, whilst they are trying to remember objects that they have at home.

It may be necessary to put some everyday objects in the room before commencing with this lesson, that is, objects that match the solid shapes (sphere, cube, cuboid, cylinder and cone).

Criteria

Adult Pre-entry Curriculum Framework for Numeracy

Measure, shape and space: shape and space

Milestone 7 – sub-element 2
Milestone 8 – sub-element 2

These elements progress to MSS2/E1.1 in the Adult Numeracy core curriculum.

Lesson S5   3D shapes in our lives

Objective

- to visualise shapes in reality situations.

> ### Resources
> - solid shapes. One of each of the following:
>   sphere, cube, cuboid, cylinder and cone.

Lesson plan

Stage 1: Introduction and class discussion

1 Place the shapes so they are in full view of each student.
2 Introduce the shapes, one at a time, and ask students if they can see anything in the room that has the same shape as the solid shape (matching).
3 Ask students if they have anything at home which has the same shape as the solid shape (visualisation).
4 Repeat the above with each of the shapes and write down the name of each of the items named by the students. This can be either on the board or on labels.

Activity

1 Use the '*Examples of 3D shapes in our lives*' worksheet, inviting students to write (or copy) the names of objects in the appropriate boxes under the shapes.

Name: _____   Date: _____

Examples of 3D shapes in our lives

Sphere	Cube	Cylinder	Cuboid	Cone
○				

S5 3D Shapes in our Lives – Worksheet
© Nadia Naggar-Smith, *Teaching Foundation Mathematics*, Routledge, 2008

Lesson S6 – Shapes in the supermarket

Tutor's notes

Check with the local supermarket when will be the best time to allow students to carry out this activity. If it is not possible to take the whole group, students should be encouraged to go with a friend or caretaker. They should all then bring the results into their class. This will promote discussion.

When discussing the findings, it will be useful to have some items from the supermarket, to demonstrate how the shapes fit together.

Criteria

Adult Pre-entry Curriculum Framework for Numeracy

Measure, shape and space: shape and space

Milestone 4 – sub-element 2
Milestone 5 – sub-element 2
Milestone 6 – sub-element 3
Milestone 7 – sub-element 2
Milestone 8 – sub-element 2

These elements progress to MSS2/E1.1 in the Adult Numeracy core curriculum.

P scales

Using and applying mathematics   P7
Shape, space and measures   P8

Lesson S6   Shapes in the supermarket

Objective

* to find shapes in everyday life.

Resources

* a few of each of the following: tins of food, boxed items, for example, tea or cereal, packets of soup, round fruit or vegetables, e.g. oranges and onions.
* one 'Supermarket Observation Sheet' per student.

Lesson plan

Stage 1: Introduction and class discussion

1   Place the items on a table, in view of all the students.
2   Hold up one item, for example, a tin of beans, and ask the students if they know what shape it is and how they know that it is that shape.
3   Repeat steps 1 and 2 with each item.

The packets of soup will create discussion, as they do not have a definite shape. At this point, students are learning to classify 'what is' and 'what is not'. They will distinguish between differences and similarities.

4   Discuss which items will stack and which will fit side by side on the shelf, without leaving a space.
5   Discuss how the oranges could be displayed. 'Will they roll off a shelf?', 'How could you stop them?'

Activity

1   Students could work individually, in pairs or in small groups to carry out the activity.
2   Each student, or group, should be given a 'Supermarket Observation Sheet' and shown how to fill it in by using crosses or ticks.

Name:_____ **Date:**_____

Supermarket Observation Sheet

How do they fit on the shelf?					
	Tidy	Untidy	Does not leave gaps	Leaves gaps	Put into a box
Dog food in tins					
Tea					
Butter in paper					
Tins of beans					
Oranges					
Cornflakes					
Sliced bread					
Jars of jam					

Lesson S7 – Stacking shelves

Tutor's notes

The faces of the items are made up of 2D shapes. This fact could be used as an introduction to 2D shapes. The linking of new work to established work helps to improve long-term memory.

This activity could be used as an alternative, or as reinforcement of the 'Shapes in the supermarket' activity in the previous lesson.

Criteria

Adult Pre-entry Curriculum Framework for Numeracy

Measure, shape and space: shape and space

Milestone 4 – sub-element 2
Milestone 5 – sub-element 2
Milestone 6 – sub-element 2 and 3
Milestone 7 – sub-element 3
Milestone 8 – sub-element 2, 3, 4 and 5

These elements progress to MSS2/E1.1 in the Adult Numeracy core curriculum.

P scales

Shape, space and measure   P6, P8

Lesson S7   Stacking shelves

Objectives

- to develop the ability to recognise the properties of 3D shapes and how they fit together;
- to introduce 2D shape.

Resources

- a variety of large cardboard boxes;
- a selection of various items such as tins of food, cereal boxes, fruit, boxes of tea, toiletries, and so on;
- a container of paint (poster paints).

Lesson plan

Stage 1: Introduction and class discussion

1   Stack the large cardboard boxes and ask the students to imagine that these are kitchen units in their home.
2   Discuss with students the best way of stacking the shelves.

Activity

1   Students may work individually, or in pairs to stack the items in the 'kitchen units'.
2   Encourage discussion on how the items will fit together on the shelves. Questions to ask:

- How steady will they be?
- Will they roll off?
- Will they fit together leaving no gaps, or will there be gaps?

3   Discuss the spatial position of the items – above, below, inside, behind, on, and so on.
4   If students are unsure whether there are gaps, ask them to dip the end of the items in the paint and then stack them on the shelves. (It is advisable to line the 'shelves' with newspaper first.) The items will leave prints on the newspaper, which can be lifted out from the 'kitchen units' and be examined in detail. Students can then see whether there are gaps or not.
5   You could also discuss the weight of the items and ask the students to decide whether the lighter or heavier items should be placed higher up on the shelves.

Lesson S8 – Investigating nets: using 2D and 3D shapes

Tutor's notes

This activity could be used as an alternative, or as reinforcement of the 'At the supermarket' activity.

The faces of the items are made up of 2D shapes. This could be the start of introducing 2D shapes.

Criteria

Adult Pre-entry Curriculum Framework for Numeracy

Measure, shape and space: shape and space

Milestone 6 – sub-elements 2 and 3
Milestone 7 – sub-elements 1, 3 and 5
Milestone 8 – sub-elements 1 and 3

These elements progress to MSS2/E1.1, MSS2/E2.1, MSS2/E2.2 in the Adult Numeracy core curriculum.

P scales

Shape, space and measure   P8

Lesson S8   Investigating nets: using 2D and 3D shapes

Objective

- to develop the ability to recognise the properties of 3D shapes and their relationship to 2D shapes.

Resources

- a few of each of the following plane shapes: rectangles, squares, triangles, circles;
- a variety of empty boxes, such as cereal boxes, boxes of tea, and so on, and a variety of cylinders, for example, Smarties tube, toilet roll tubes, Pringles container;
- fruit, for example oranges or tangerines;
- some poster paint and paper;
- 'Investigating nets: 3D and 2D shapes in our lives' worksheet.

Lesson plan

Stage 1: Introduction and class discussion

1   Draw 2D shapes on the board (or prepare a chart in advance of the lesson). The shapes are a rectangle, a square, a triangle and a circle.
2   Ask students if they can name any of the shapes on the board/chart. Encourage the correct naming of the shapes.
3   Pass the plane shapes around and encourage the students to discuss the properties of each shape and to match them to the shapes on the board.
4   Ask questions like: 'How many sides does the shape have?', 'How many corners?', 'Are the edges straight or curved?'
5   Place the empty container items on the table and ask students to identify the 3D shapes.
6   Hold up one of the boxes and ask the group what they think the container will look like if it was flattened out.
7   Demonstrate how the boxes could be opened out and laid flat on the table.
8   Talk about the 2D shapes that have been made by dismantling the boxes.

Activity

1   Students may work individually, or in pairs. They each select a box to work with.
2   Assist students to carefully open up the box and see what shapes they can identify.
3   Instruct students to draw the shapes on a piece of paper or to identify them by matching them with the plane shapes that were examined in part one of the lesson. The shapes to be identified are rectangles, squares, circles and some triangles (depending on the type of packaging being investigated).
4   Assist students to record their results on the worksheet 'Investigating nets: 3D and 2D shapes in our lives'.

Additional activity

This activity may be a bit messy, but fun for the students.

1   Ask the group what they think the peel of an orange will look like if it was removed from the orange in one piece.

2   Invite the students to try it and see.
3   Have a competition to see who can peel the orange so as the peel remains in one complete piece.
4   Discuss what happened and examine the shapes made by the orange peel.
5   All eat the oranges!

Name: _____ Date: _____

Investigating nets: 3D and 2D shapes in our lives

Type of package	How many circles?	How many squares?	How many rectangles?	How many triangles?
Cornflakes packet				

Lesson S9 – Measuring right angles

Tutor's notes

When students have made a right angle for themselves they enjoy checking that their right angle matches their neighbours.

  When students notice the fact that, although the two pieces of paper may not match in shape and length, the right angle corners *will always match*, this strengthens the concept.

Criteria

Adult Pre-entry Curriculum Framework for Numeracy

Measure, shape and space: shape and space

Milestone 8 – sub-element 1

This element progresses to MSS2/E2.2 in the Adult Numeracy core curriculum.

P scales

Shape, space and measure   P8

Lesson S9　Measuring right angles

Objectives

- to measure right angles in lives;
- to measure right angles in shapes.

Resources

- a piece of paper approximately A5 size (scrap paper or newspaper is fine);
- 'Right Angles in Our Room' worksheet;
- felt tip pens or pencil crayons, blue, yellow, green and red (one set for each student or between two students).

Lesson plan

Stage 1: Introduction and class discussion

1 Start the lesson by explaining to students that they are going to be working with right angles today and asking if anyone knows what a right angle is.
2 Depending upon the response, you could explain that a right angle is a 'square corner' and demonstrate this by running your hand around the corner of a table.
3 Draw the attention of your students to the fact that the corners of a square and the corners of a rectangle are right angles.
4 Instruct students on how to make a right angle from their piece of paper:

    a 'Fold your paper any way you like, but only make one fold.' (The edges do not need to meet.)

    b 'Now fold it again and you will make a right angle.'

Activity

1 Students work in pairs, measuring angles to find which are right angles.
2 They measure walls, cupboards, books (anything they like) and discuss the results.
3 If they wish to record a few (or all) of their results they may use the worksheet on 'Right Angles in Our Room'.

Name:_____ **Date:**_____

Right angles in our room All of these have a right angle (square corner):